PORTRAIT

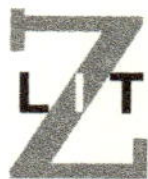

Sara Guyer and Brian McGrath, series editors

Lit Z embraces models of criticism uncontained by conventional notions of history, periodicity, and culture, and committed to the work of reading. Books in the series may seem untimely, anachronistic, or out of touch with contemporary trends because they have arrived too early or too late. Lit Z creates a space for books that exceed and challenge the tendencies of our field and in doing so reflect on the concerns of literary studies here and abroad.

At least since Friedrich Schlegel, thinking that affirms literature's own untimeliness has been named romanticism. Recalling this history, Lit Z exemplifies the survival of romanticism as a mode of contemporary criticism, as well as forms of contemporary criticism that demonstrate the unfulfilled possibilities of romanticism. Whether or not they focus on the romantic period, books in this series epitomize romanticism as a way of thinking that compels another relation to the present. Lit Z is the first book series to take seriously this capacious sense of romanticism.

In 1977, Paul de Man and Geoffrey Hartman, two scholars of romanticism, team-taught a course called Literature Z that aimed to make an intervention into the fundamentals of literary study. Hartman and de Man invited students to read a series of increasingly difficult texts and through attention to language and rhetoric compelled them to encounter "the bewildering variety of ways such texts could be read." The series' conceptual resonances with that class register the importance of recollection, reinvention, and reading to contemporary criticism. Its books explore the creative potential of reading's untimeliness and history's enigmatic force.

PORTRAIT

Jean-Luc Nancy
Introduction by Jeffrey S. Librett
Translated by Sarah Clift and Simon Sparks

Fordham University Press

New York   2018

"The Look of the Portrait" was originally published in French as Jean-Luc Nancy, *Le regard du portrait*, copyright © Éditions Galilée, 2000. Simon Sparks's translation was previously published in English as "The Look of the Portrait," in Jean-Luc Nancy, *Multiple Arts: The Muses II*, 220–47, copyright © 2006 by the Board of Trustees of the Leland Stanford Jr. University. "The Other Portrait" was originally published in French as Jean-Luc Nancy, *L'autre Portrait*, copyright © Éditions Galilée, 2014, and appears here for the first time in English.

This work received the French Voices Award for excellence in publication and translation. French Voices is a program created and funded by the French Embassy in the United States and FACE (French American Cultural Exchange). French Voices Logo designed by Serge Bloch.

Fordham University Press has no responsibility for the persistence or accuracy of URLs for external or third-party Internet websites referred to in this publication and does not guarantee that any content on such websites is, or will remain, accurate or appropriate.

Fordham University Press also publishes its books in a variety of electronic formats. Some content that appears in print may not be available in electronic books.

Visit us online at www.fordhampress.com.

Library of Congress Control Number: 2018933435

Printed in the United States of America

20 19 18 5 4 3 2 1

First edition

Contents

Preface to the English-Language Edition

> "The portrait often seems to be the action or expression of its cause (which is the subject, or the model); it is a space entirely rooted in the subject."
>
> —Jean-Louis Schefer, *Figures peintes*

The portrait is suspended between two extremes: On the one hand, it tends toward likeness, and on the other, toward strangeness. On the one hand, it identifies, and on the other, it distances. The first side is that of proximity, recognition, description, and illusion; the second is that of distance, questioning, suggestiveness, and encounter.

One could say that presence is the shared border of those two extremes. Presence is itself an ambivalent theme: Either we imagine it as a full reality, immediate, and closed upon itself, or else it is thought to be the coming, the approach, or the opening of an alterity. It is either a question of what is called a representation in the ordinary sense of the term (a copy, a *fac-simile*), or else it is a presentation, a gesture that invites or suggests. Either the image disposes or it proposes.

This is why the art of the portrait has always been more or less clearly divided between two regimes of judgment: either a judgment about exactness, or one about forcefulness. A portrait is either faithful, precise, serviceable for identifying an "individual," or else it is powerful, expressing dynamics by means of which "somebody" advances and withdraws. This art has always oscillated between an administrative or policing technique and a meditation on the infinity of a face.

The first of the following essays is devoted to the latter meditation. It seeks to consider how the art of the great portraitists makes something appear in the look of their "models" that gets eclipsed or that vanishes into the infinite—plunged into the distance, or else into the "spectator's" own look. So there remains neither model nor spectator: There is rather the proposal or the possibility of an encounter and of what, within an encounter, will always lose its bearings beyond it.

The second essay asks what happens to the portrait when representation (imitation, figuration) is no longer bound by the requirements of exactness and recognition. Indeed, the contemporary portrait is no longer committed to the possibility of recognition even when it has a person's name in its title (or even if it is designated as a self-portrait). Even a smear can be designated as a "portrait." Nonetheless, it remains the case that this simple designation invariably opens up the call or appeal of a search, an expectation, or a tension: What look arises from this image? Or else, how does this shape look? (And we know straightaway that "looking" not only involves the eyes but an entire arrangement of features, volumes, and surfaces.)

The portrait is certainly not about to disappear. To the contrary, it is appearing in a truth that is becoming all the more acute. It questions more. It demands a renewed thinking, a revitalized feeling for what is happening with the human figure. If the portrait attests to the fact that this figure is disappearing right in front of us in the world that we make for it, at the same time it also reminds us that disappearance belongs to appearance, and distance to the approach of presence.

Jean-Luc Nancy

What is the subject of the portrait? Nothing other than the subject itself, absolutely. Where does the subject have its truth and validity? Nowhere else but in the portrait. That is why there is only a subject in painting, just as there is only painting of the subject. In painting, the subject sinks to the bottom (it "returns to itself"); in the subject, painting surfaces (it exceeds the face). Thus emerging from out of a line, neither subject nor object but art, or the world.

Introduction
The Subject of the Portrait

Jeffrey S. Librett

In the two essays published here, Jean-Luc Nancy reads the art of the portrait in terms of an ontology of the subject while construing the subject's being in terms of its artistic portrayal. He argues that subject and portrait are to be inscribed in each other, and he sketches in broad strokes the intertwining histories of each. In Nancy's portrait of portraiture, the history of portraiture (which he illustrates with a selective *Ahnengalerie*, or gallery of portraits) gives us access to a history of the subject, and the converse. While Nancy's depiction of these histories remains just a sketch, it provides a rigorous conceptual orientation for both art-historical and philosophical discussions of the portrait and its subject.

From an Ontology of the Subject to (the) Art(s)

Whence his ontology of the subject? As most readers familiar with Nancy's work will surely agree, the most important of the many nineteenth- and twentieth-century philosophical influences on his work, as far as an ontology of the subject is concerned, is Martin Heidegger. In these essays on the portrait, as elsewhere in his writing, Nancy follows in part but also reworks Heidegger's sustained dissatisfaction with the Cartesian cogito, the subject of rational self-certainty.[1] According to Heidegger, Descartes understands the being of the Cartesian subject, a thinking "thing," only from the outside, as it were, i.e. as the being of an enduringly, fully present entity (*Vorhandenes*, in Heideggerian parlance). Indeed, Heidegger argues that Descartes constructs the ego, which is supposed to exemplify finite thinking substance, on the model of extended substance, despite his distinction between *res extensa* and *res cogitans*.[2] The tradition of the Cartesian subject of knowledge thus fails to explore and describe what subjective existence is "really like"—its appropriate ontology, which would start with an acknowledgement that any subject is originally (rather than secondarily) inscribed in its world (Heidegger's "being-in-the-world"). Such worldliness is constituted further by the subject's involvement in space and time, in relationships with objects of use (things that are "handy"—*Zuhandenes*), and in relationships with others ("being-with").[3] Heidegger rejects the language of "subject" and "subjectivity" because it is embedded in a philosophical tradition that provides an inadequate account of what "subject" purports to name. This tradition creates unwittingly the double distortion of inadequately distinguishing the subjective being from objective being, and at the same time of exaggerating and reifying the subject's separateness from things and other people in the world.

Nancy has extended and displaced this Heideggerian critique of the subject in numerous essays and books, in dialogue with close contemporaries who likewise worked enthusiastically but critically in the wake of Heidegger—most notably, Jacques Derrida and Maurice Blanchot, as well as Philippe Lacoue-Labarthe (with whom Nancy coauthored a number of significant studies), and more distantly Jacques Lacan and Emmanuel Levinas, to name just a few. Nancy tries to think through in new contexts Heidegger's thesis that the "essence of the human being lies in its existence," an existence that is always involved with a world and hence spatially, temporally, conceptually, and affectively displaced with respect to itself. More specifically, Nancy has stressed that existence involves *radical plurality and relationality*, self-alterity and self-deferral in *relation* to others. In this sense, he goes beyond the limits of Heidegger's work, which has often been criticized for having overemphasized (despite Heidegger's acknowledgement of the ineluctability of being-with-others) a heroically authentic solitude at the expense of human relationality, and for having thus failed in part to escape from the very conception of the isolated, worldless self that Heidegger had found so objectionable in the Cartesian tradition.[4] While Nancy retains the use of the term "subject"—rather than adhere to the taboo Heidegger placed on this word, a word Heidegger wanted to see replaced by his own manifestly ontological term "being-there" (*Dasein*)—Nancy nonetheless remains in some respects close to Heidegger's analysis of *Dasein*. For example, he conceives of the subject as maintaining a constitutive relationship with its own inessentiality and its own *absence*, as necessitated by the radically spatio-temporal character of existence, which defers and displaces self-presence in crucial ways. Nancy's "subject"—far from being immediately present to itself in its own self-certainty—is what he at one point here calls "the absence-subject [*l'absence-sujet*]" ("Recall"), thereby implying a certain synonymy between "absence" and the "subject" itself. But the absence is, of course, not an absence pure and simple. The being of the subject in Nancy is a "being-toward-itself" rather than a self-coinciding "being-itself." It does not occupy simply the position where it is (or where it posits itself) in time and space, but remains *ex-posed* to both otherness and absence (of the world as also of itself). In what follows, we shall see that this determination of existence as *exposition*—which combines Heideggerian motifs with an emphasis on (among other things, sensuous) being-in-relation that Heidegger, with his concern for a heroically solitary authenticity, would have been loathe to endorse—is central to Nancy's theory of the portrait.

Before retracing that theory, a few words on Nancy's approach to the arts in general are necessary. One will want to know something about how Nancy construes the relationships between portraiture (within the visual arts) and the arts in their entirety, and in turn how he construes the relationship between the arts and an ontology of the subject. For Nancy's claim that the history of portraiture gives us access to a history of the subject as a history of human being-in-the-world seems to give art a particular ontological privilege, and to give the visual arts, and portraiture in particular, a peculiar privilege within the realm of art. Yet while art does retain such a privilege, the impression that visual arts or portraiture would receive a further privilege is somewhat misleading.

In the first chapter of *The Muses*, "Why Are There Several Arts and Not Just One (Conversation on the Plurality of Worlds)," Nancy develops the notion of the singular plurality of (the) art(s). He will later elaborate this notion in a more general fashion as "Being Singular Plural" in the essay of that title. According to this "singular plurality" of (the) art(s), there is, on the one hand, no art except as the plurality of the particular arts, whose finite number remains indeterminable. On the other hand, each art form, even as it emphasizes one or more specific sensuous modalities (sight, hearing, and so on), registers the virtual presence of the other modalities within the sense or senses it highlights: "Each sensing touches on the rest of sensing as that which it cannot sense" (Muses, 17). In this way, any given artform is not just isolated in its own space but remains in a co-constitutive relation with the others it excludes. Any artform consequently stands for all arts, indeed for the whole of art, with the proviso that this whole only exists and can only present itself in the form of its (partial) absence, i.e. in its fragmented and, in principle, infinite multiplicity.

The relation between (the) art(s) and being-in-the-world is mediated by the sensuous embeddedness of each. For being-in-the-world, too, is always sensuous. Nancy suggests that the subject is always in "touch" with its world because he construes sensuous relationality as epitomized by touch. Touch is the one sense that summarizes what all senses do: They expose us to the world. The function and significance of (the) art(s), then, is to highlight the touch of sensuous being, to intensify and bring to awareness the subject's being-in-the-world. "Touch forms one body with sensing, or it makes of the sensing faculties a body—it is but the corpus of the senses. . . . . . [A]rt touches on the sense of touch itself. . . . It deals with being-in-the-world, in its very springing forth. . . . as exteriority and exposition . . . that are formally grasped, isolated, and presented as such" (*Muses*, 17–18). To follow how Nancy works out this approach to (the) art(s) with respect to a broad spectrum of the particular arts, we would have to read his writings on portraiture in connection with those on painting and drawing and these together with others on music and poetry.[5] As this obviously exceeds the scope of the current Introduction, suffice it to have indicated here the outlines of his ontological approach to the working of (the) art(s), and the conceptual context of his approach to the visual arts more specifically.

Nancy's essays on the art of the portrait involve two components—a generalizing (or structural) dimension and a historicizing (or narrative) gesture. While these two components are intermingled to some extent, "The Look of the Portrait" presents a more structural view of the portrait as such, whereas the "The Other Portrait" is largely concerned with a historical sketch of the (subject of the) portrait. Since G. E. Lessing's *Laokoön*, we tend to think of visual arts (prior to film) as synchronic and mimetic, whereas we construe literary ("poetic") and musical arts as diachronic and diagetical. Given this conventional schema, the two dimensions of structure and history that are in tension in Nancy's essays evoke the tension between spatial and temporal arts. Moreover, as we shall see, the tension between spatial and temporal dimensions is one that Nancy will situate at the heart of the portrait itself, thereby disrupting the schema we inherit from Lessing (among others). This is one way, and perhaps even the principal way, in which Nancy's account of the portrait situates in this artistic modality the artistic modalities of music and poetry to which, according to his theory of (the) art(s), the visual arts necessarily relate by way of manifest exclusion.

The Portrait of the Exposition

In "The Look of the Portrait," Nancy sees the portrait as attempting to bring to light not the identity of the model (or of the painter) but "the structure of the subject: its subjectivity, its being-under-itself, its being-within- and so its being-outside-, behind-, or before-itself. . . . its ex-position" ("The Autonomous Portrait" in what follows). The subject that, according to Nancy, is to appear in the portrait does not coincide with itself except as this paradoxically singular non-self-coincidence and multipositionality that the word "ex-position" is called upon to capture.[6]

As this ex-position is neither a simple objective given nor a pure self-positing subjectivity, and as it involves and includes the ex-position of others (principally the artist and the spectators), its presentation can be neither merely active nor merely passive. Ex-position is the mode of active-passive being of the subject as an interiority that "takes place within" ("The Autonomous Portrait") exteriority. Nancy writes accordingly that the portrait must "produce the exposition of the subject" but also that it must "bring it forth, . . . draw it out" ("The Autonomous Portrait"). Production here is *poiesis*.[7] The ex-position of the subject of the portrait is not simply the painter's construct, nor the pure self-expression of the model, but the result of a middle-voiced occurrence involving artist, model, and spectator.

The structure of the portrait's subject as exposition further gives the portrait what Nancy calls its "autonomy," but in an unheard-of, ironic sense, displacing both the art-historical conception of the "autonomous portrait" and the broad aesthetic notion of the modern "autonomous" artwork. Here, the portrait's "autonomy" signifies that the portrait is "the putting (in) to (the) work of the *autos* or of the *self*, of *being-to-itself*" ("The Autonomous Portrait"). As such, it signifies exposition: The portrait is the "putting (in) to (the) work of exposition" ("The Autonomous Portrait"), including that of the viewer and painter, who are exposed to the portrait as the portrait exposes the exposition of its subject.[8]

Nancy reduces the portrayal of exposition to three dialectically interrelated aspects or dimensions: *resemblance, recall,* and *look* (or *regard,* or *gaze* [*le regard*]).[9] Insofar as the question of resemblance plays itself out on a synchronic axis of substitution, it is implicitly a spatial dimension; because recall or remembrance operates on a diachronic axis of combination, it constitutes or occupies a temporal dimension; and because the look combines resemblance and recall in the very (absent) center and basis of the portrait, as well as its (abyssal) end, we can think of the look as a figure for the portrait's cause (efficient and/or final). Further, in terms of implicit allusions to the registers of Jacques Lacan—which Nancy at once evokes and holds at a distance, reformulating them here in his own terms—resemblance concerns the imaginary of the portrait, recall involves the symbolic (presentation of the absence of the thing), and the look suggests the Lacanian dimension of the real, specifically the object (a) as cause of desire.[10] Finally, as indicated previously, the aspect of resemblance alludes to the visual arts in their concrete referentiality, while the aspect of recall (which implies also anticipation) alludes to the musical and poetic arts in their nonsignifying radical narrativity, and the dimension of the look (which escapes the view, as we shall "see") suggests the musicality of the visual and the visuality of the musical, in their very impossibility.

Nancy approaches *resemblance* by displacing traditional notions of the portrait as the likeness of a model that would capture the essence of his or her identity. The portrait does not resemble the essence (nor the appearance) of its model as an objective thing, for the subject of exposition is no given object or fully present entity. Rather, the portrait resembles the subject only insofar as the subject is in a relation of self-resemblance to its (never arriving) self. This self-resemblance is not that of an inert thing (*Vorhandenes*). It is a "being for itself" ("Resemblance"), rather than "in itself." The "portrait" thus resembles a being-in-relation (to itself and/as others): It "resembles 'resembling itself'" ("Resemblance")—at once its own and that of its "model." In this sense, the portrait can only resemble the model to the degree that the model (like the painter) resembles him- or herself (and also remains unlike him- or herself). Portraiture is thus inscribed in the subject, while subjectivity is inscribed in the portrait, as the (im)possibility of self-resemblance.

While Nancy characterizes in terms of resemblance the quasi-spatial and imaginary interplay between identity and difference in the portrait's self, he construes in terms of memorial *recall* the temporal and symbolic interplay between identity and difference. It is with this latter dimension of recall that Nancy addresses the question of re-presentation while foregrounding the role of absence in any re-presentation. That is, while we traditionally think of a re-presentation as the presentation of an object or thing in its absence, i.e. the restoration of its presence despite its absence, Nancy shifts this notion in a small but critical way. He understands the aim of the portrait as the presentation of the presence of the very *absence* of the subject. For subjectivity in its very presence always maintains a fundamental relationship with its own absence, both future and past. The portrait "is the presence of what is absent, a presence in absentia . . . charged . . . with presenting presence insofar as it is absent: with evoking it (invoking it, even) and with exposing it, with manifesting the retreat in which this presence is maintained" ("Recall"). This is so because the subject itself is marked radically by such absence: "The invention of the subject consists in the invention of an infinite movement of absention, the absolute measure of the return or the turn to oneself (to the other). It is this subtraction from the presence of the object, this access to the absent character of the subject [*l'absence-sujet*], that commands the portrait . . ." ("Recall"). The portrait therefore does not re-call into the presence of the picture (or its beholding) the prior presence of the person (understood either as immediate self-presence or as immediate presence before another). Rather, the portrait re-calls the subject's process of re-calling itself to itself in the self that is always to come, and specifically, always to come into the world that it already inhabits. As the portrait resembles (self)resembling, so the portrait recalls (self)recall: "the act of recalling oneself that constitutes the subject in general" ("Recall").

The third, "dialectical or logical" (n24, "The Look of the Portrait") moment of the portrait is what Nancy calls the *look*, or *gaze*. By this he means, first of all, the look or gaze of the person portrayed in the image, but also the look of the artist and the look of the spectator gazing upon that gaze. None of these looks can actually manage to reach or gain access to each other (or to themselves). In Nancy's very rich analysis of the look as the very center and epitome of portraiture—which he characterizes in turn as the center and epitome of visual art tout court—the gaze is without object: It looks at nothing, and disappears into the "absence of the subject" ("Look"), the very core of subjectivity. In this sense, it is its own (nonobjective) object.[11] The look "carries the subject forward" or "brings the subject to the fore [*porte le sujet en avant*]" ("Look"), in a simultaneously spatial and temporal sense. It moves out of the self and back into the self, out toward resemblance and back toward recall. And what it sees is only the (non)appearance of the nothing of the thing in itself ("Look"). For the look is the "thing in itself of a departure from the self through which alone the subject becomes a subject" ("Look"), as "opening toward a world" ("Look").[12] In sum, the portrait brings into focus "the ontological problematic of the subject in the whole extent of its constitutive distension and the entire tension of its ambivalence. On the one hand—presence to itself—closure in the work, the sovereign figure, the glorification of vision and the face; on the other—presence set outside itself—the gesture and the touch of painting, the figure gone astray, the look lost in the rhythm of its own capture" ("Look").

The Withdrawn Other of the Portrait: A Historical Sketch

The title, "The Other Portrait," was not Jean-Luc Nancy's invention. Rather, *L'altro ritratto* (which, as he explains, can mean both "The Other Portrait" and "The Withdrawn Other") was already the title of an upcoming exhibition of contemporary portraiture when Nancy was asked to write the catalogue essay by the Director of the Museo de Arte Moderna e Contemporanea di Rovereto e Trento, Cristiana Collu, in 2013. The exhibition was held in Rovereto from October 2014 to January 2014. In his essay, "The Other Portrait," Nancy takes as his point of departure the ambiguities of the Italian title, and develops further the view of the portrait's structure that he had developed in "The Look of the Portrait." Here, he sketches the outlines of a historical account of portraiture in connection with an abstract narrative of the subject's main phases in the West.

Beginning with classical Greece, the development of an explicit concept of mimesis creates the conditions of ancient secularization under which portraiture is possible and necessary. "Mimesis" inaugurates the attempt to seek "in the man and in the human world, a witness to the enigma (mystery, divinity, force, sacrality) that other cultures are going to look for in typified human forms (through a hieraticism or a symbolism), be they animal, vegetable, mineral, or "abstract" (motifs that are geometric, wavy, etc. . . .)" ("Mimesis"). Mimesis, according to Nancy, does not personify the gods allegorically or embody them in human appearances, but rather, it "brings forth the divine presence in an appearing that is the appearance of man" ("Mimesis"). Instead of representing the gods, a portrait portrays a self (and in this sense all portraits are "self-portraits"), an *autos* that is autonomous first of all in the sense that it is no longer dependent on the gods of myth, who have withdrawn. (At this point, Nancy is evidently elaborating on his discussion of the "autonomous portrait" in "The Look of the Portrait.") And yet this autonomous self now takes on the "full force" and the "whole enigma" ("Mimesis") of the withdrawing gods. Through this human supplement of the divine, "the divine appears in the resemblance of the human form to itself" ("Mimesis"). The divine thus appears as a subject in the sense of what is not "a simple thing, but . . . always already in itself a relation, the relation-to-self" ("Withdrawn Presence") that constitutes the self. The fact that a relation-to-self involves self-difference is already part of the structure of the self here, but it becomes entirely manifest only in modernity.

Having recalled the traditional (and with particular relevance, Hegelian) notion that the subject begins to emerge in the West with Greek antiquity, Nancy recognizes that it develops in radically new ways throughout the constitution of Christianity and, subsequently, in Renaissance humanism. Through this development, the self-sameness of the self continues to be its explicit touchstone, but at the same time, Nancy emphasizes, the self-sameness of the self as a relation-to-self continues to imply self-alterity (without which there could be no relation). Now, however, the divine otherness that appears (invisibly) in the human face is the otherness of the nonrepresentable Judeo-Christian God. Moreover, as the activity of representation comes to be increasingly understood as situated in a subject, all representations (generated by any subject) come to represent, to those who perceive them, their own self-representational activity. Representation in the form of portraiture becomes the imitation of a self-creative self-imitation (for example, as self-expression) that exists in its model, its artist-creator, and its spectator, all of whom participate in creative activity to the degree that they are made in the creator-God's image. But at the same time the portrait becomes in an exacerbated manner the "representation of an un-representable" ("Ipseity") because the God-like self-relation (which is the core of the self) does not appear as such in any particular imitation or expression of itself.[13] The self-as-relation withdraws and absents itself from each of its representations, whether these are accomplished by another self, or by itself (as other). The divine "alterity beyond reach" ("Ipseity"), as absolutely creative self-relation, reappears in the supplement of human selfhood.

In the wake of the Reformation, beginning roughly with Rembrandt, from the seventeenth to the twenty-first centuries, the alterity of the self, which had always been *implicitly* presupposed by the notion of the autonomous subject as a self-relation, becomes both *explicit* and increasingly detached from any divine instance. The invisible core of the portrait begins to assert itself within or against the visible image, while conversely the image is mobilized against its ideal content. Prior to the work of Rembrandt, Nancy argues, the withdrawal and becoming other of the subject in the portrait had always signaled (or been read as) a "mystery," in the sense of a "process of unveiling" in which the subject appeared in the half-light of the veil, holding "in reserve a superior clarity" ("Revelation"). One still finds the representation of such a "divine light," he suggests, in Dürer's Christlike "Self-portrait at Twenty-Eight Years Old Wearing a Coat with a Fur Collar' from 1500. But starting with Rembrandt, this transcendent mystery previously promised by the portrait is gradually replaced by an "enigma" in which the half-light of the veiled appearance of the mystery becomes undecidably split between a "still divine possibility and another for which the 'human' is no longer self-evident" ("Revelation"). The "uncanny" and the "grotesque' replace the "mystery"—Nancy's principal example here is Goya—as "realism" develops, in the sense of "the mimesis of an opacity, indeed, of an impenetrability of the real" ("Revelation").[14] This displacement of portraiture both registers and exacerbates an alteration of the subject. The subject becomes 'obscure … confused." It loses its halo (the "presence deep within the subject" ["Divine Abandonment"]), according to Charles Baudelaire's prose poem that Walter Benjamin made famous again in the criticism of the twentieth century with his thesis regarding the loss of the aura in modern art. Or it appears as the series of skulls Cézanne painted toward the end of his life.

In the radicalization of this situation, during the first half or two-thirds of the twentieth century, painting distances itself at once from figuration and (perforce) from the human face—from figure as symbolic expression of the soul. Having lost faith in the full self-presence of the model, mimesis achieves its autonomy at the moment when the very meaning of this "autonomy" as self-positing presence dissolves. Representation comes to represent itself, becoming its own "subject" where there is no longer a subject to represent nor a subject as creative source of representation.

The final stage in the history of the portrait that Nancy attempts to characterize is the contemporary moment, from the late twentieth century into the early twenty-first. This is, after all, the moment that his catalogue essay is meant to situate in historical and conceptual terms. Disfiguration, overfiguration, or effacement of the human figure and face become, in the contemporary portrait, the order of the day. And yet—surprisingly—the portrait insists in the midst of the negativity of this disfiguration. It seeks to convey there an otherness within and beyond the otherness of the divine, which had been transferred to the human subject across the ages of Judeo-Christianity and its humanist inheritance, and which is no longer plausible. A withdrawal of the other and an otherness of the portrait play themselves out in new ways (as illustrated particularly by the works of Fautrier and André Kertesz). Given this insistence of the figural portrait, the tendency to disfiguration appears for Nancy as transformative, involving the search for "a transfiguration that . . . denotes the burst of a presence taken aback in absence, of a passing, of a dream where not the 'fulfillment of a wish' but the real of a desire in action [*le réel d'un désir en acte*] can be recognized" ("Dis-figuration"). After all the transcendences have been exhausted, the human face, centered in its abyssal gaze, still "obstinately demands another recognition of alterity that it feels itself to bear and without which . . . it could not attain the minimum of ipseity or selfhood needed to exist" ("Dis-figuration"), a fleeting presence that cannot be situated or fixed. In contemporary arts of the portrait, therefore, one seeks less "a sameness or identity than . . . an alterity or alteration of the identical" ("Eclipse"), the subject as "an appearing of disappearance" ("Eclipse"). The absent subject of the portrait presents itself there as an otherness or alienation, an unnameable disturbance or perturbation, the look of the other portrait as it withdraws from view.

The Look of the Portrait

How passionate had been our desire for thought, if it had granted us so clear an image of itself to look upon.

—Plato, *Phaedrus* 250d

The Autonomous Portrait

> The only words of Rembrandt's that we know are these: *I have done nothing but portraits.*
>
> —Matisse, *Écrits et propos sur l'art*

A portrait, according to the standard definition or description, is the representation of a person considered for him- or herself. This definition is as correct as it is straightforward. All the same, it is far from being sufficient. It defines a function or a finality, that of representing a person for him- or herself and *not* for his or her attributes or attributions, for his or her actions or for the relations in which he or she may or may not be involved. The object of the portrait is, in the strictest sense, the *absolute* subject: the subject detached from everything that does not belong to it, withdrawn from all exteriority.

(Ultimately, the question that I shall want to ask here will be nothing other than this: What is it to paint the absolute? And so: What is absolute painting?)

Clearly, however, any such finality is going to demand a whole range of clarifications. What do we mean by "person" (individual, subject, particular, *quidam*, "someone," whatever name we choose)? And what do we mean when we speak of a person "for itself," as neither character nor personality, but *for itself* without extension or restriction? As we can see, the very design of painting a portrait involves all these sorts of questions, the entire philosophy of the subject.

What is equally clear, however, is that any such definition, which addresses only the object of the portrait (of its *subject*), ignores the work that the portrait ought to be, the technique or the *art* that ought to allow for the working out of its design.[1] In view of this, then, another definition needs to be added: "The portrait is a painting organized around a figure."[2] Yet we still need to clarify precisely how such an "organization around" is able to lead properly—organically—to a "figure" that is not simply the center of attention but also understood as that of a subject being considered for itself. (To take a well-known example, Watteau's *Indifferent* is organized around a figure without actually being a portrait; at least that is what its title would suggest.) The concern here, therefore, should really be with the properly pictorial marks imposed or raised by this sort of compositional design, with the traits proper to the portrait and with that of which such traits treat in painting, with what they draw from it and put on display.

The parallel between these two definitions mirrors in large part the genre of painting itself. A painting is organized around a figure insofar as this figure is itself the real end or goal of representation to the exclusion of any other stage [*représentation*] or scene, any other representational stake or value, any other evocation or signification.[3] The true portrait, then, is what art historians have tended to place within the category of the "autonomous portrait," in which the character being represented neither is caught up in any action nor bears any expression that might otherwise divert attention from his or her person. Perhaps we could say that the autonomous portrait should be the impression of—and should give the impression of being—a subject without expression.

So far as action is concerned, there is, no doubt, only one sort that is in any way admissible here: the action of painting itself, which often appears in self-portraits and sometimes in portraits of one painter by another.[4] In fact, the action of painting is one whose representation constitutes both a turning back in and a doubling of the *subject* of the painting.

As such, the portrait does not constitute simply a revelation of an identity or a "me."[5] No doubt this is always what is being *sought*, the overriding end of imitation thus comprising a revelation (an unveiling that would draw the *me* from out of the painting, something, then, that we might term an "uncanvassing"). And yet this can only ever be the case—if it ever *can* be the case, and it is precisely this faculty and this possibility that are at stake here—on the condition that it brings to light the structure of the subject: its sub-jectivity, its being-under-itself, its being-within- and so its being-outside-, behind- or before-itself. On the condition, then, of its ex-position. The "unveiling" of a "me" can take place only by acting on this exposition, putting it to work, as it were. To paint or to figure is no longer to reproduce, therefore, not even to reveal, but to produce the *exposition of the subject*. To pro-duce it: to bring it forth, to draw it out.

The figure being portrayed ought to organize the painting, therefore, not only in terms of balance, lines of force, or color values, but also in such a way that the painting is absorbed into it and completed by it. What surrounds the figure—if, indeed, it is surrounded by anything—ought to be strictly subordinate to its pure and simple position for itself. A *self* in and *for* itself: such is the exclusive concern of the portrait. As is well-known, moreover, this is the exclusive concern of thinking from Descartes (or from Augustine) right up to today (or until tomorrow). The extent to which these two concerns are, in fact, *the same* is precisely what is being asked here. Once again.[6]

It might well be, indeed it might legitimately *have* to be, that there is nothing surrounding the figure and that the "organization" of the painting tends toward the straightforward detachment of this figure from a monochrome ground [*fond*], which largely equates to an absence of ground. This sort of situation is not exactly uncommon, although it is certainly never frequent. The face can emerge from the shadows but, within a particular setting, it can also bring to the fore that aspect of shadow that lies at the center of the look; in each case, the stakes are *visibly* the relation between a boundary and an opening, between an orbit and a hole. Something revolves around this look. It is not enough that the painting organizes itself around a figure; this figure must itself be organized around its look—around its vision or its clairvoyance. What does it see? What does it have to see? What does it have to look at? Such is the central question of my remarks here.

And yet the figure has to be detached or isolated in such a way that it does not consume the entire canvas if the contours of the face are not to be dissipated and the gaze turned inward, something rather different from painting's purpose.[7] So, the figure, the whole figure and nothing but the figure, because it is the figure as a whole and not the eye in isolation that effects the look.

Of course, there is nothing to prevent the portrait from showing the rest of the body so long as its sole function is to carry the face, so long as it remains, in short, in reserve, a resource on which the look can draw. The body is most often reduced to its upper part, with or without the hands (which doubtless have their part to play in the organization of the subject) and, except on very rare occasions, to the line formed by the shoulders. What this glimpse of the clothes tells us is that the body is not naked. Indeed, a face that hinted in that direction would displace the entire intention of the portrait. Whatever the link between a naked body and the face, nudity involves stakes that are not, or not exclusively, those of the subject, not of the "person" but of nudity for itself (albeit the nudity of the person).[8] Indeed, we could perhaps go so far as to say that the portrait marks a break with nudity (without repressing it) because it exposes another sort of nudity altogether, that of the subject.[9]

Of course, it is always possible for there to be more than one figure or for this figure to be plural. Giorgione is known for being one of the inventors and masters of the so-called "double" or "triple" portrait, and there are, in one or two very rare cases, portraits with as many as six or seven figures, occasionally even more.[10] What is most remarkable, however, is that the characteristic of a plural portrait is always the mutual avoidance of looks; the looks neither meet nor seek one another out. The characters are devoid of relation. Their common presence in the painting instead constitutes a sort of diffuseness or resonance (in musical terms, a canon or a fugue) with regard to the motif of the subject. Their looks should be without mutual regard,[11] sharing nothing but their mutual autonomy.

Whence, then, the identity of this autonomous figure? Most often from the title: *Portrait of Ugolino Martelli*, for example.[12] Sometimes the name figures in the painting itself, although this is a somewhat archaic and rare device; at other times (as we shall see a little further on with Gumpp's *Self-Portrait*) it is bound up with a specific intention. In which case, however, it tends to be accompanied by an inscription relating either to the glory and merits of the person depicted[13] or to the truth or fidelity of the representation itself,[14] to the glory of (the) painting, if you prefer, to the glory of its autonomy.

It would be possible to analyze at length all the possible variations on these identifying statements, which run from the exteriority of a name outside the painting right through to the painting's inclusion of a self-reference: Ultimately, however, it is always a matter not (or, in any case, not *only*) of a painting's reference to the real person it represents, but of the general form of a self-relation, a relation that is as much that of the proper name in its nonsignificance as it is that of painting posed as truth. To put it differently, referential identity and pictorial (autonomous or self-referential) identity are asymptomatically linked to one another—unless it is from their initial identity that the portrait first proceeds.

In the first or last instance, the identity ultimately given outside the figure is merely that of *the figure itself*. And this is also why, in addition to portraits titled by a name, there are just as many portraits titled along the lines of *Portrait of a Young Girl*, *Portrait of an Old Man*, or simply *Old Woman* or even *Head of a Man*, and so on. Referential identity either remains extrinsic or is identified with pictorial identity. The social position of the portrait is its figural position. This, however, can be understood in either of two ways:

1. When the portrait moves in the direction of social position, when it becomes referential and descriptive (when it becomes a portrait designed for the recognition, in every sense of the word, of posterity, of the people, of the family, even of the police, as has sometimes been the case), the identity of the person lies outside it, and pictorial identity, by conforming to referential identity, is lost.[15]

2. Painting gives itself its own "social" position; it engages its own civility or sociality, and it is perhaps only through it and in it, moreover, that subjects

enter into a relation between *subjects* and not of identificatory objects. In other words, the horizon of our questions is in no sense solipsistic; on the contrary, it is one in which the portrait is always the portrait of another in which, however, the value of the face as the *sense* of the other is truly given only in the portrait (in art).[16]

The identificatory image relates to its model. The portrait relates to itself alone, for it relates to the self alone: to the self as other, the sole condition for there being something like relation.

As such, the portrait attains its artistic dignity only by being, in traditional terms, a portrait of the "soul" or of interiority, not *rather than being* a portrait of outward appearance, however, but *in the very place of* this appearance, in its place, the place of its appearance manifested on the painter's canvas. The portrait of Giovanna Tournabuoni by Ghirlandajo bears the following inscription: "Art, could you only represent [*effingere*: render and produce, express and execute, draw out and fashion] character and spirit, there would be no more beautiful painting on earth."[17] This exhortation goes for all portraits and for all painting; understood correctly, it involves more than a mere wish and more, too, than the feeling of insufficiency that a wish would evoke, because it does not call for *another* painting but states, rather, that *this* painting ought to be able to be seen as bringing into view *mores animumque*. Along with the painter's humility, perhaps, it is the assurance of his or her design that invites us to look upon a soul *in* or *on* the figure that he or she presents.

The portrait's identity is wholly contained within the portrait itself. The formal "autonomy" of the figure involves nothing less than the autonomy of the subject that is given *within* and *as* it, as the interiority of the two-dimensional canvas and so as the autonomy of painting that alone *makes up* the soul. The person "in itself" is "in" the painting. Devoid of any inside, the painting *is* the inside or the intimacy of the person. It is, in short, the subject of its subject, its support and its substance, its subjectivity and its subjectility,[18] its depth and its surface, its sameness and its alterity in a single "identity" that we call the *portrait*. (Beyond this, perhaps, we would call it *painting* in general because no painting can ever be "soulless," as it were, and so devoid of "subject" any more than it could be devoid of "figure," *even when* it is an "abstract" or a "monochrome." We can't stop the extension of this double questioning; if every subject is a portrait, then every painting is perhaps a figure and a look.)

The subject of the portrait is the subject that the portrait itself *is*; both insofar as the portrait is the subject (the object, the motif) of such a painting and insofar as this painting is the place at which such a subject (person, soul) comes to light. Either that, or the subject of the portrait is the subject that is a subject insofar as it comports itself *to itself* ("self-present"), and it only does so to the extent that it is what comes back to itself from outside the canvas, from the inside out, maybe, the slight surface of painted canvas being nothing other than the interface or the exchange of this being-to-self.

Hegel, of course, both protested—with what was, for his time, genuine insight—against the debasement of the portrait as a genre and saw in it the true completion of painting.[19] This completion (which, for Hegel, is also the median completion of art in general: painting is the midpoint between exteriority and interiority) stems from the expression of "inner life" or "spiritual character." Hegel understands this "expression" as a translation or a reproduction of the life of Spirit through the skill of the painter; not just any painter, therefore, but the "hand of a master" (Titian, for example). The secret of this hand—the secret of good imitation—is knowing how to produce a lively rendering of what makes up the life of Spirit. As such, it is life *itself* that is being recognized and reproduced. In a sense, we need add nothing to Hegel's considerations since they are more than enough to explain the singularity of the artist. Still, they fail to measure up to art in the truth of its execution or its exteriority. Paradoxically, the very materiality and technique of the portrait are set aside (Hegel fails to deal with any particular portrait) in favor of a *mimesis*, the concept of which imposes both the difference of an original from a copy and the identity of a pure self-expression of the life of Spirit.

Without wanting to pursue any further the (aporetic and/or dialectical) question of this double self-*allo*-mimetic allocation,[20] let me recall that, in failing to dwell on the portrait itself (in failing to wonder exactly whence or how the "expression of Spirit" comes to be *figured*, and in failing, too, to ask what this *life* exactly is), Hegel also fails to dwell on an essential trait of the process of spirit (and thus of its life), the fact that it is nothing other than self-relation mediated through a departure from the self. This is the real cross that any dialectical thinking has to bear: either the moment of exteriority (negativity) exists in and for itself, or it is merely negated in turn. (Which is why, moreover, art is the cross that any such thinking has to bear.)

If we really want to dwell on the moment of exteriority and hold firmly to its *autonomous* existence, the logic of a contradictory mimesis dictates that we will also have to hold to another, more advanced logic, one that means we will be asking no longer how the portrait comes to be the portrait of the subject but how the portrait is itself the execution of the subject. We shall be asking no longer how painting comes to represent Spirit but how it *presents* it, how it presents what will never have been present elsewhere. Granted, this is not going to be possible without making some weighty decisions as to dialectics and, first and foremost, as to the claim that exteriority is not just a moment but the very substance, support, and surface of the subject "itself," thereby suspending the dialectical return to the self or making of it something undreamt of by any thought of the subject, even though everything about that thought would seem to lead in this direction: to wit, the relation of the portrait to its audience.[21]

With the invention of the portrait, the subject does not give itself the pleasure of an image; instead, it assures itself of the certainty of a presence (its "own"); it has invented itself. (Another way of putting it would be to say that pleasure and certainty here are the work of one and the same joy.)

Somewhat more profoundly—or more superficially (here, it is much the same thing)—than any imitation of the face, the portrait involves a particular relation from the outset; that it does so is the most basic trait of painting. And this is what allows us to say that painting has a particular way of *setting out* [*un* abord], that it *sets out* toward us, and that this way of setting out stems from all painting (from its essence, if you like) and is communicated to all its works and to all its genres.

The "autonomy" of the portrait shelters it from every relation to a particular setting or scene only in order to set it immediately into a relation that is simultaneously unique and exclusive *and* endlessly renewed, a relation to the subject and to the subjects to which it is presented or exposed. Exposition is neither an appendix nor an ostentation of the quality or essence of the portrait, but wholly of a piece not only with painting but even more, were this possible, with the portrait. "Interiority," as I have already said, takes place *within* "exteriority." "Exposition" is this *setting within* and *taking place* that is neither "interior" nor "exterior" but *set toward* or *in relation*. We might say that the portrait *paints exposition*, that it *puts it (in) to (the) work*. Here, however, "work" does not refer to the particular "painting" as an object or thing. Rather, it refers to the painting *as relation*. In this sense, then, it is *the subject* that is *the work of the portrait*.

The portrait paints a subject only by setting itself within a subject-relation; as such, it sets a putative subject (me, you, the painter) within a relation to the subject that is being exposed. It sets a subject within a subject-relation and so within a relation to self. The portrait is the subject of a subject that lies before (or behind) it. But how so, and whence this relation that constitutes the very being of the subject (if a subject can be said to be a being-for-(and through)-another-subject)?

It has often been said that every portrait is a self-portrait and that *ogni pittore dipinge sè*.[22] Without wanting to deal with the various ways in which this phrase (which relates, moreover, to every genre of painting) might be interpreted or with the respective merits of such interpretation, I still want to point to the fact that such a remark is indissociable from its opposite: Every self-portrait is first and foremost a portrait. In fact, the circumstances that lead the painter to put himself in the position of model (circumstances that could well be based on pure convenience, unsatisfying though such an explanation may be) change nothing essential as regards the real concern of the portrait, to wit: its being not the representation of a subject but the execution of subjectivity or of being-self as such. Its *autonomy* has to be understood, beyond the technical sense of the term, as the putting (in) to (the) work of the *autos* or of the *self*, of *being-to-itself*. The portrait relates to itself alone; to put it differently, it is nothing other than this relation.[23] Yet this is so only precisely insofar as it is exposed to us; it is the putting (in) to (the) work of exposition, *our* exposition, our being-before—and only thus within—ourselves.

The relation that makes up the portrait comprises three moments: the portrait resembles (me), the portrait recalls (me), the portrait looks (at me).[24]

Resemblance

> It gradually becomes clear that a portrait does not resemble
> because it looks like a face; rather resemblance begins and
> exists only with the portrait and in it alone; resemblance is the
> portrait's work, its glory or its disgrace, expressing the fact that
> the face is not there, that it is absent, that it only appears by way
> of the absence that resemblance precisely is.
> —Maurice Blanchot, *Friendship*

If resemblance appears to be the overriding concern of the portrait, it ought to follow that it constitutes the paradigm of representational or "figurative" art. Everything that revolves around the figure of the portrait, that binds it to the problematic of representation itself, all concerns this particular art.

The portrait appears dedicated to the job of resembling. So much so, indeed, that it might as well be seen as the only genre of painting that has a clearly determined practical finality. And it is around just such a finality, moreover, that judgment as to its artistic dignity has been meted out. (In this context, we should bear in mind that, across the field of art, the portrait is the genre that most emphatically bears the trace of a function or a service: an *hommage* or service to truth that is never too far removed from a sense of religious service. Yet what is so remarkable about this is that the portrait is also quite distinct from the religious icon. This problem involves the whole atheological autonomy of art; I will come back to it in due course.)

It is this impericus desire to resemble a particular individual that has left the portrait in the contrasting—if not wholly contradictory or oppositional—position of being seen as both the work of a jobbing artisan and the pinnacle of the art of painting. (Even today, and despite the advent of photography, quick portraits attract tourists and flaneurs alike, as if satisfying our need both for recognition and for seeing something emerge manually, as it were, and not out of some sort of recording device. "It's him, it's really him!" we cry, repeating once again that most traditional of *doxa*, very often adding, in a phrase that seems to cry out for extended commentary: "You'd half expect it to speak.")[1]

Yet as we already know, if the identification of the particular model is essential to any portrait that is meant to be recognized,[2] the same cannot be said for the *art* of the portrait. So much so, indeed, that we can quite legitimately claim that the model is wholly inessential to the portrait; more exactly, that the model is what is essentially absent, that its absence and *not* its being recognized is what matters most. Resemblance has *nothing* to do with recognition. With the large majority of portraits that we see, we never get to see the originals, and it is hardly by chance that the identity of the Mona Lisa, the archetypal portrait, is still so uncertain, as much as to its gender as to the sense or inflection of its smile (indeed, it is precisely this uncertainty that has given it its legendary place). And we can even admire portraits that, in their own time, were judged wholly unsatisfactory from the point of view of recognition.[3]

+

Consider Johannes Gumpp's self-portrait (circa 1646) (Figure 1).[4] Its rather odd composition has lent it a certain notoriety. Like many self-portraits it is devoted less to the representation of a particular person than to the representation of the act of process of representation itself. What is being painted is less the painter than *painting*. Painting is the subject of this painting, in every sense of the term. It is, quite explicitly, the subject of its own resemblance.

The painter or the painting paints the entire scene, a scene that involves two different representations of the painter's face, the face in the mirror in which he becomes his own model, and the face on the canvas that he is in the process of painting.[5] The resemblance is twofold; there are two distinct resemblances. The painting shows the dissemblance of resemblances.

The image in the mirror and the one on the canvas are identical (the portrait, like the mirror image, being reversed: have a look at the lock of hair) except for their respective looks: The look cast by the face in the mirror looks at the painter who looks at *himself*; the look thrown by the portrait is to one side, restoring thereby the movement of the eye that the painter has to make in order to switch from the mirror to the canvas. As such, the look of the portrait no longer looks at *itself* but looks instead at the one who is looking at the canvas and so at the painter in the process of painting; the "same" who becomes thus the "other." With the same "stroke," however, it looks out on us, the painting's prospective audience. The look of or in the mirror is fixed on the original or model, the original or model of or in the painting looking out onto the painter/painting.[6]

Where is the real resemblance, therefore? In the mirror or in the portrait? The painting gives us the answer in the form of the two domestic animals

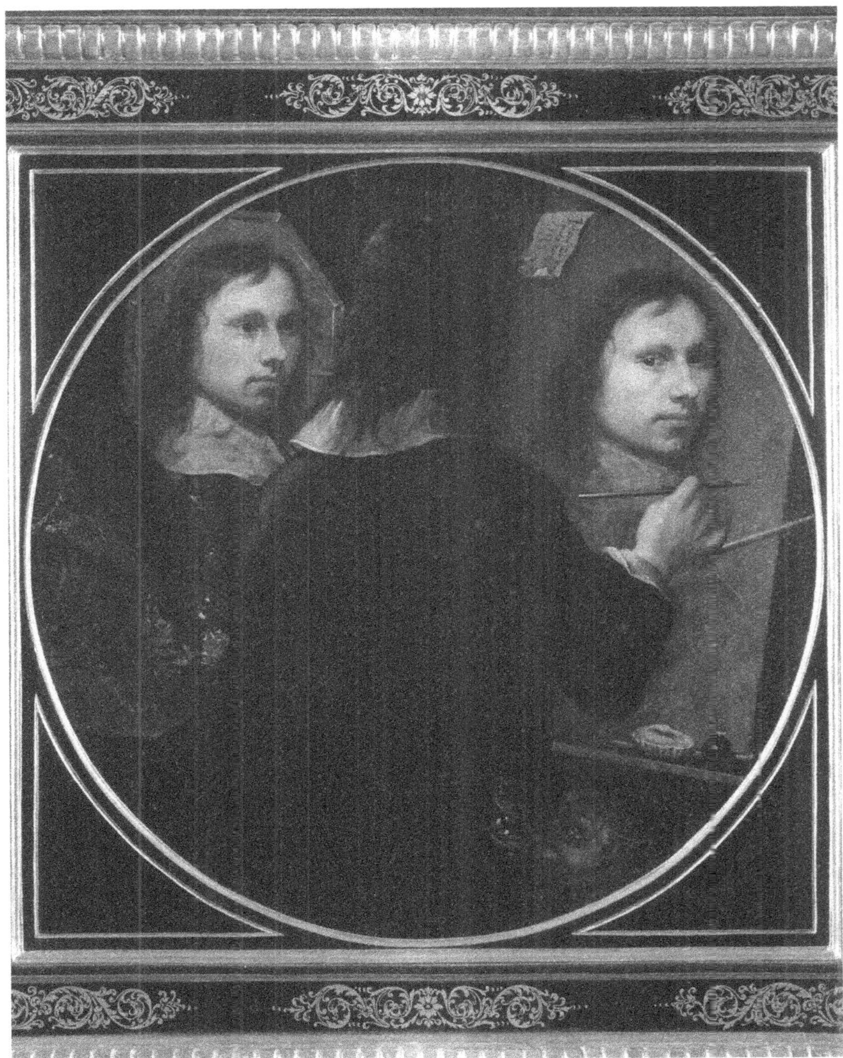

Figure 1

set furiously against one another: the dog, placed under the portrait and in the foreground, symbolized fidelity,[7] while the cat, beneath the mirror and further back, indicates, if not infidelity, at least a less precise or less vivid sort of fidelity. (As if to draw out the difference further, the name "Johannes Gumpp" is written on the piece of paper placed at the top of the portrait.) If the mirror is indeed less faithful, it is because the formally exact resemblance that it provides (leaving aside the inversion) is still not the resemblance afforded by painting. And since it is not a matter of redressing the mirror's inversion, the difference has to stem from the difference in looks. The look in the mirror is only concerned with itself, engaged as it is in nothing more than a purely technical attention. By contrast, the look of the portrait is directed elsewhere, looking out for the look thrown its way, looking out for an undefined possibility of attention or encounter. As such, it mobilizes, through one or two discreet traits (to say nothing of the difference in lighting), the whole face before finally showing a person rather than the traits of a model. Faithful resemblance consists in showing something quite different from a correspondence between traits.

Now while this sort of resemblance does indeed show the life or the liveliness of Spirit, as Hegel puts it, it does so only by revealing itself to be the art of painting itself. A few details underscore this (re)presentation of art: while the mirror, flanked by a bottle whose reflections point ultimately to the purely mechanical character of reflection, reflects part of the studio, the painting itself is accompanied not only by two of the painter's tools (the diluting shell[8] and the flask) but also by a flute (the portrait doesn't speak; art makes itself heard) and a rosary hung beneath it (a gesture of gentle mockery or sulfurous devotion? or a metaphor of reverent contemplation?).

The mirror shows an object: the object of the representation. The painting shows a subject: painting at work.

In the portrait—in painting—there is no *object*; nothing is *thrown out* [ob-jeté] before us. In this sense, the painting is never placed *before* us. It is not "before" but "ahead" in the sense in which it is I who is behind or within the painting, in its presence. Even this, however, what we might call the painting's intimate presence, is not defined and given before the painter like an image in a mirror, like a model in the studio. It is not a model but an Idea. Yet this Idea is nothing other than the Idea of painting itself. It does not preexist painting; rather, it is carried out by painting. The "Idea" of art is only ever art itself, and it is different each time.

The opposition of representational conformity and resemblance in painting is far from unimpassioned. Not for nothing are the cat and dog set at each others' throats. They are two forms of passion snarling at one another in defiance (the only audible noise on this little stage on which it is the role of the flute to modulate the eloquent silence of art). We might say that whereas one is the narcissism of reflection,[9] the other is the passion—simultaneously more passive *and* more active—of the self's relation to the other or to the self as other. The reflection (or the double) happens only *in praesentia*. The portrait is *in* absentia; it is essentially and in every sense exposed to absence.

Gumpp's painting, however, presents something else: ultimately nothing less than the painter himself, a third resemblance that leads us to say: this one is the right one.

It is the painter himself who, in the act of painting, occupies the foreground of the canvas. It is the painter who sums it all up in the gesture of the hand armed with brush (charged with the red of the lips), doing so in such a way that the hand, along with its arm, might almost be incorporated or, indeed, incorporate itself into the painting that it is in the process of painting, as if painting itself were painting the canvas. If we leave the hand to one side, all we can see of the painter is his back and a tumble of dark hair highlighted and situated by the white collar, which captures the light. The dark back of the painter, the back of his look, as it were, the mere reflections and effects of which peer out at us, this shadow much like the one spoken of in the fable of the birth of painting, this dark mass turned toward us and laid down before our eyes as a challenge to pictorial conventions, this is what ultimately harbors resemblance in its extreme truth, exposing it as an absence. (In much the same way, Vermeer's *Painting* shows us the painter from behind while placing a mask on the table.)

In truth, however, we are still not finished; all this could be painted by another painter who might well paint this entire scenario set before him, doing so without ever seeing the face of the first painter, who would still remain masked.[10]

This absence shows us that the painting resembles only insofar as it exposes this absence, an absence that, in turn, is nothing other than the condition under which the *subject* relates to itself and so *resembles itself.* "Resembling oneself" is nothing other than being oneself or the same as oneself. It is this very sameness that the painting paints. But this sameness is the endless referral of a look cast on the self to a look turned outside itself and to an exposition of itself. This sameness extends all the way to the unrecognizable identity of a dark back turned toward me as if it were my own and as if I were myself the surface of the painting, my face thus before that of the painter, *my face as invisible as it always is to me.* In the first or final instance, the resemblance of the portrait relates to the absence of the face, its being-before-itself.

I can "resemble myself" only in a face that is always absent from and outside of me, not like a reflection but like a portrait brought before me, always in advance of me. The portrait portrays this advance and this movement before, this keel that, in the stream of what lies without, opens the thin and quickly erased wake of a "self."

As such, the painting resembles insofar as it resembles a "resembling itself," and the portrait resembles insofar as it "resembles a portrait" (as Pontévia remarks) and so insofar as it resembles itself, sameness is identified with painting, in painting, and as painting.

It does not resemble an original;[11] rather, it resembles the Idea of resemblance to an original or is itself the "original" of the resemblance-to-self of a subject in general, a subject that is each and every time singular. It is in my portrait or my portraits alone that I can learn, if I need to, of my "sameness." And each one of my portraits will identify yet another resemblance.[12] In a bad portrait, the separate elements of representation are not focused into the unity of a resemblance and constitute a mere enumeration of traits. In a good portrait, resemblance mobilizes each one of those traits in order to draw them toward that absence—simultaneously "inside" and "outside," behind and before the painting—of which resemblance is both the semblance and the arrangement.

In Matisse's portrait of Auguste Pellerin (the one dating from 1917) (Figure 2),[13] a long black swathe is drawn out from the painting that hangs behind the painter's face, spilling over its frame so as to melt into or layer onto the bedrock of the portrait itself, a black background in which even the painter's clothes will be lost in order to bring to the fore, before the frame that surrounds it like a halo,[14] the face whose oval shape explicitly sets it apart, while two black eyes open, eyes through which the ground of the portrait (that of resemblance) may be seen, but through which it also *sees itself*.

In bearing a resemblance to a particular person and to a particular side of that person, a portrait does not thereby resemble someone or something, unless it be resemblance itself or the particular "person" insofar as that person resembles him or herself. By resembling itself, it is itself, that is, an identity *for itself* and not for another thing *in itself*. Painting paints the for-itself and not the in-itself; this is clearly something very different from how painting is usually understood since painting or portraiture means in the first instance, *drawing out* [tirer],[15] and so a drawing out of the "in-itself" (which has, properly speaking, stifled itself, been stifled by its nocturnal ground, the very identity of a "to itself"). Resemblance is *drawn* from the obscure and unidentifiable identical.[16]

It is not a matter of reproducing something recognizable, therefore, any more than it is a matter of giving phenomenal appearance to something that would otherwise remain buried, "grounded," as it were (the in-itself as the "life of the mind," as "personality trait," etc.). Rather, it is a matter of drawing out the ground itself, of drawing presence not out of absence but, quite the contrary, toward the absence that brings it before "itself" and exposes it to self-relation by exposing it to a "we."

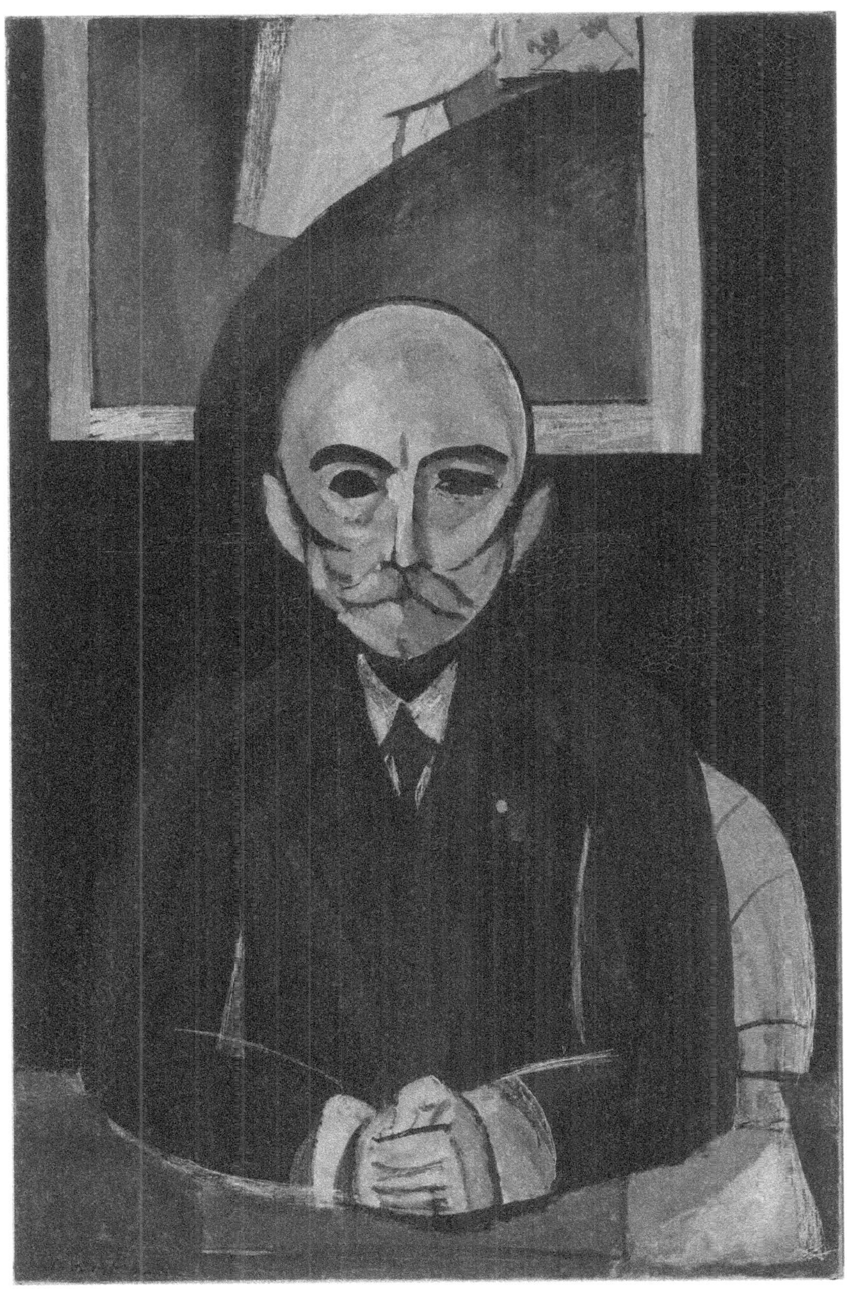

Figure 2

By keeping quiet about the essential silence of the plastic arts and by carrying this silence forward through the visible mark of a mouth (Gumpp's touch of red on each of the mouths and on the brush, the pinched, narrow mouth of Matisse's Auguste Pellerin),[17] the mouth of the portrait opens (and closes) onto an obscure ground: It exposes a sense that is in no way a signification, something that could be articulated, but is instead the articulation of presence or the *pre-sense of presence* itself.

Recall

Images of images, shadows drawn from a past "dream of
shadows," paintings; with them, we cross shadows and dreams—
the shadow in which death gathers its forces, the dream in which
life is condensed—so as to return to the magically addressed
starting point: a look that is neither a question nor an answer but
silence and a pause, a mute witness to what was.
—Jean-Christophe Bailly, L'Apostrophe Muette

The role of the portrait is to look out for [guarder] the image in the absence
of the person, regardless of whether this absence results from distance or
from death. It is the presence of what is absent, a presence in absentia that is
charged thus not only with the reproduction of characteristics but with the
presenting presence insofar as it is absent; with evoking it (invoking it, even)
and with exposing it, with manifesting the retreat in which this presence is
maintained. The portrait recalls the presence in both senses of the word: it
brings back from absence, and it remembers in absence. As such, then, the
portrait immortalizes; it renders immortal in death.

(A more exact way of putting it might be to say that the portrait is less the
immortalization of a person than the presentation of (immortal) death in (a)
person. And therein would lie the essential difference between the portrait
and the death mask, which presents the dead and not death as such. The mask
takes the imprint of the dead (the work struck by death), while the portrait
puts death itself (in) to (the) work: death at work at the very heart of life, at
the very heart of the figure, in full view. Death in this sense denotes what can
be addressed under the concepts of "finitude" or "division": the departure
from the in-itself, ek-sistence, ex-position.)

The Roman portrait, both of ancestors and of illustrious figures, is the
first moment of the portrait proper and, along with the medallion, is what
provides modernity with one of the principal models for the portrait.[1] At
the same time, with the formation of the Christian subject (and so of the
subject per se) and of another relation to death and to absence (to an absence
opened right within the *interior intimo meo*), we see the Oriental or Christian

version of the Greco-Roman portrait in the portraits of Fayoum and their "mute cries."[2]

Love, death, and glory all communicate in one and the same movement of absention: they withdraw from ordinary presence, from the presence of the object, from its existence [*l'être-là*]. They put being outside itself; thrown thus, it moves toward itself. The invention of the subject consists in the invention of an infinite movement of absention, the absolute measure of the return or the turn to oneself (to the other). It is this subtraction from the presence of the object, this access to the absent character of the subject [*l'absence-sujet*], that commands the portrait and explains why love, death, and glory were the principal sponsors of the portrait before it turned to the denuded subject, portrayed for itself, and to the painter and the act of painting: painting indefinitely recalling itself to itself. What I am here terming a "recall" is the recollection to oneself of a presence that has managed to absent itself.

The act of memory that I want to evoke is not the conversion of a present that has passed on; rather, it is the step or the move back toward the always-present—and properly immemorial—ground of absence itself. This anamnesis, in some way hypermnesiac (or amnesiac), refers back to the region of absent presence that was once called the sacred. The portrait takes on the somber glow of this region in which presence exceeds itself as it moves more originally from itself to itself. This is the "divine" excess (in Augustine's phrase) of originary interiority as an unclosable yawning; an identity infinitely constituted "for itself," and that is also to say: "for the other."

There is nothing surprising, then, in our saying that the *princeps* document of the history of the subject (of its presence and its presentation) is a seminal literary portrait—*The Confessions*—in which a subject represents itself through the act of presenting itself to God and through the act of presenting the nonpresentable character of God as the ultimate truth of His face.[3]

This "divine" or this "sacred" is nothing other than a distancing and hollowing out through which contact with the intimate is to be made, through which the passion of its infinite interiority/exteriority—the passion of sufferance and the passion of desire—is to be broached. It is the rupture necessary to self-communication, to the communication of the self. And in this sense, then, every portrait is "sacred."

Rather more precisely: The movement from the icon to the portrait is exactly that from divine presence, offered in the face of its own absence (for which words are not lacking because it is itself the movement of the Word and of the Spirit), to a "desacralized" figure, that is, a figure opened onto the silence of its own absent presence. So far as this presence is concerned, it is a matter of drawing out its trace in every singular face. We need not, therefore,

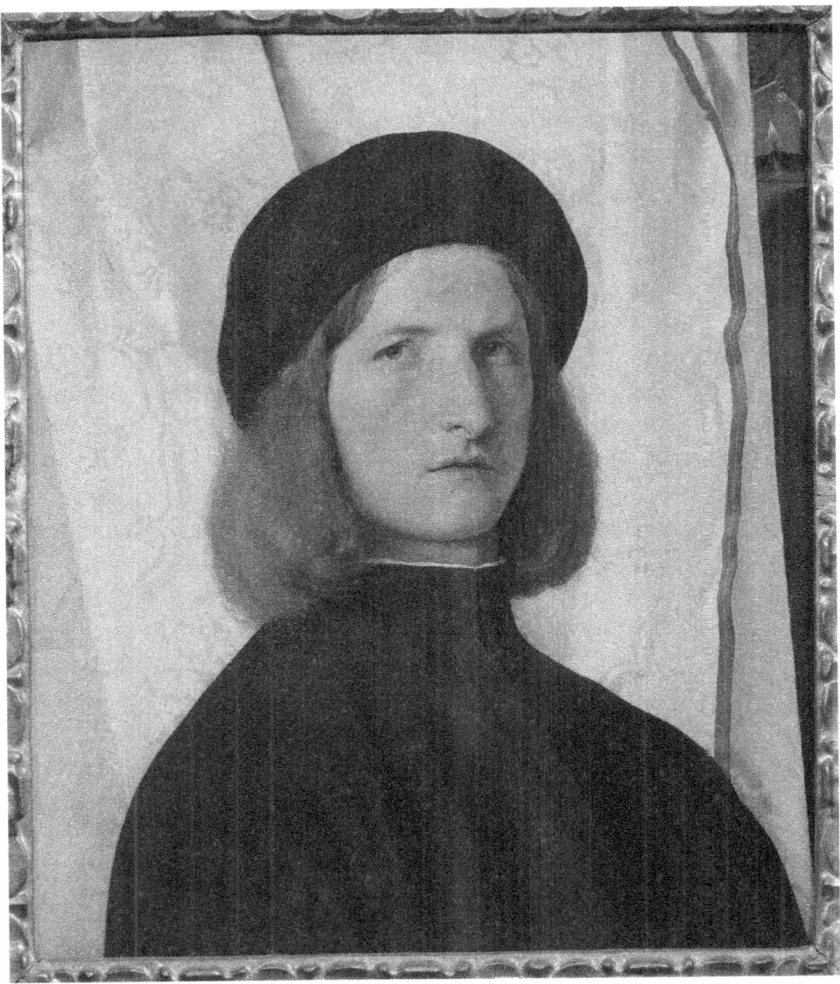

Figure 3

speak of the "sacred"; rather, it is simply a matter of drawing out the trace of presence, of drawing or recalling the intimate trace of its passion. Presence is *portrayed* [*on la* pour-traict] (as the original French term has it), *drawn to itself*. And this is no less true of painting.

Take Lorenzo Lotto's portrait of a young man (Figure 3). A first glance immediately demonstrates the "iconic" character of this image, which is presented, moreover, as an inversion of the shadowy scene of Gumpp's canvas. The cap and hair are fairly close to a sort of inverted halo against the golden background—the decorated decor—of the vast damask curtain. Everything here, as in thousands of other portraits, denotes the model's excellence and so reveals why he merits being kept and thus held present in his absence. Just what this absence entails, however, we will never know,[4] any more than we will know whether the reason behind the painting is love, death, glory, or all three—or even a wholly different reason, the model perhaps having here (as might be suggested by the absence of any name) no other function than that of being a model.

The absence of any marked social standing immediately confers on portraits of this sort what we might call a state of pure distinction. On the one hand, the resemblance is that of a well-determined individual (overdetermined, one might say, by some of the details, the mole in the middle of the forehead being only the most obvious, but there are other details on the skin and in the precise fold of the upper of the scarcely parted lips); on the other hand, it is a resemblance that cannot be identified except as a resemblance to itself. Now, in resembling itself, it principally resembles its own withdrawal into itself; this is nothing other than presence itself, its *praes-entia*, what puts it before itself and so renders it capable of coming back to itself. The withdrawal into its "interiority" is wholly up to the challenge of the precision of its physical "exteriority," each one incessantly passing into the other.

By evoking the past presence of a handsome face, simultaneously lively and reserved, almost shy or evasive (evading what, though? identification? confusion?), this figure of a young man recalls not an individual but the act of recalling onself that constitutes the subject in general—an act that, for this very reason, never takes place "generally" but only in an irreducibly and endlessly singular fashion that is continually being renewed.[5]

We could say that this young man offers what is, in some way, a quasi-aggressive exhibition of his intimacy. Through his air of defiance, through the calm bravado that projects a certain tension out onto the spectator who would seek to uncover his secret, he also poses—by holding the pose that he does—the possibility that his intimacy might concern us (that it might look toward us). He *distinguishes himself*, then, in every sense of the term, but, in doing so, he forces us to recall this distinction. The withdrawn, the distinguished, is a secret, the secret of intimacy; yet this intimacy is not a secret jealously guarded by the young man, held "back," as it were. He merely exposes it and draws it out.

In point of fact, there is no "back" here. "Back" means "beside"; there is no side to the "self." The only side is the visible side of the canvas, which, as we know, is devoid of depth. Intimacy is the game of a depth that belongs to no other ground than the surface on which it is played out and stretched out. Again, then, what is being stretched is the passion of a subject in thrall to that mode of being-itself in which it relinquishes its hold on itself while both exposing and communicating itself in an almost violent way. (As Bataille remarks, the sacred is nothing other than the communication of the passions.) In Hegelian terms, we might say that this young man is wholly in-himself-for-himself but is so only insofar as he is *for us*.

The portrait is less the recollection of a (memorable) identity than it is the recollection of an (immemorial) intimacy.[6] Identity can always be past, whereas intimacy can only ever be present. Once again, however, the portrait is less the recollection *of* this intimacy than it is a calling back to it. It calls us or summons us to it or toward it, leading us there; through the painting that is offered up to our look, we enter into the manner in which it is presented to the outside.

Now, if we look closely, we can see how the painter has arranged things in such a way as to draw our look. The curtain rides up on the right side of the canvas, as if the painting were revealing its ground, its "back" or flip side. In the upper right-hand corner, where the vast, luminous curtain is most visibly folded toward us, we can see, in the background, as it were, the room in which the painting is being painted. In this dark corner there shines, somewhat unusually, a lamp, an oil lamp whose flame flickers feebly while reflecting on its copper supports.

Commentators have often tended to refer this lamp—as unusual as any number of Lotto's symbolic details—to John's *lux in tenebris lucet*. To my mind, however, the allusion to the Gospel is not really necessary once we understand that, in a strictly atheological way, the light is precisely the light of the young man's intimacy. Not, however, in the sense that the painter would be suggesting or allegorizing the idea of an inner light (although it is certainly possible that that was indeed his intention), but much more in the sense that this lamp, painted straight onto the canvas, is itself the material or pictorial luminosity of the intimacy in question. This shadowy flame doubles the young man's look, forming thus the look of the painting itself. So, far from simply leading us symbolically outside the painting and into the depths of a soul, it also brings us back to the immanence of the canvas and the painting. Or, if you prefer, it shows us that the ground of the soul takes place here and nowhere else, in this withdrawal that is thus drawn forth.

If this were not the case, what use would painting have? It would be far more useful to tell the story, whether fictional or real, of this young man and his concerns. Painting is not an allegory of the soul or of spirit. In no sense is it the imitation of an interiority that would be given to it from somewhere else, of the life of an Idea or of a person. Rather, it is the execution of the figure of just such an interiority and is so precisely insofar as it is not a matter of an interior that one might ultimately be able to see behind a particular figure. The portrait did not appear in order to recall the memory of cherished or admired lives (the portrait is not a monument and, when it is, it is already well on the way to being a portrait no longer).[7] It appears in order to recall the subject to itself, in order to bring about its infinite return to itself.

The portrait does not recall a distant present; rather, it brings absence closer, so close that its call is silent. Never was a soul or a spirit as close to itself and to us; never did it call on itself as well as on us.

The light of the ground—of this improbable ground that opens groundlessly in the ground of the canvas—is the shimmer of a presence before and beyond itself, a presence that calls it*self* forth.[8]

If the portrait does indeed give rise to and hold within itself exactly such a gesture of the recollection and anticipation—this deceptive and redemptive promise—of a presence equal to its absence, it is because it provides the repository and the emissary of the collapse of the divine into absence that lies at the very heart of monotheism or, more precisely, of the monologotheism whose path the "West" will have been. Every portrait plays out in the singular the impossible portrait of god, his retreat, and his attraction [*son retrait et son attrait*].[9]

In fact, monotheism is characterized less by the unity of God (as if it were a matter of a simple numerical reduction) than by the essential propriety of this unity—what basically grounds it as a unity—namely, indivisibility. The plurality of the gods constitutes their visibility, whether potential or actual, as well as their presence. The art of polytheism provides a vision of the gods,[10] while that of monotheism recalls the indivisibility of God withdrawn into His unity. Whence, as we know, the Judeo-Islamic edict against representation[11] and, most singularly, against the portrait, as well as, in a matter both parallel to and consequent on this, the enormous importance of the intra-Christian debate around images, from the Council of Nicea to the Counter-Reformation.[12]

The art of the icon[13] is the art of a negative and apophantic theology. It is an art that denies representing what it presents. The icon exposes the invisible, not by rendering it properly visible but by exposing the presence of the invisible, calling thereby for a vision other than that of sight. The invisible God is not simply situated away from our eyes; rather, He is invisible in and for Himself, and this is why it has always been possible to think of Him as being invisible to his Son, thus making the latter an "invisible image of the visible."[14] In truth, the one God is less invisible (in the sense of being hidden) than nonappearing; far from being a matter of making this nonappearance appear (this nonappearance considered as the very act of God His *modus operandi*, so to speak), it has to be a matter of presenting its presence, which is itself absence. Equally, the iconic figure is not a visage but a face; it exposes the nonappearing face of the whole of the visible.

The portrait will have retained one fundamental trait of the icon, however: What it *draws* and *traces* is precisely this nonappearance as the birth and death of the subject. At the very point where the icon offers itself up to the adoration that cuts through it so as to move toward the ground of the divine, the portrait offers instead the sight of ground becoming surface as the proper illumination of the painting. In this way, Matisse's *Auguste Pellerin* can be said to refer simultaneously, and more dryly or with a tension far greater than that generated by Lotto's *Young Man*, to a particular person, to painting, to the form of the icon, to the overflowing of ground in the setting out of the foreground, to a subject charged with the concern and gathering of it*self*.

The portrait recalls the icon and resembles it in much the same way as the absence of presence recalls, so as to resemble, the presence of absence. It recalls, in the finite character of each, the infinite distension of the *one*.

Look

> This "look" expresses what, precisely? Its exercise: its regularity,
> its particular kind of constancy … the ground no longer masks
> the person to which it lent the alibi of a history, of a fiction,
> of both a distant sense and a role. It seems that this is what the
> portrait continually repeats: the fact that there is no longer
> any attested or organized sense but, above all, no longer any
> delegation of sense.
>
> —Jean-Louis Schefer, *Figures peintes*

The light of the portrait shines from its obscure ground. It shines from out of the star, eclipsed for itself, that defines a subject. What visibly disappears in the portrait, what, under our very eyes, hides itself from our eyes, plunging into them as if to infinity, is the look of the portrait.

Before anything else, then, the portrait looks; looking, it is concentrated, both sent and lost. Its "autonomy" gathers and restricts the painting, even the entire face, in the look; this look is the goal and the site of this autonomy.[1] Painting the look does not mean imitating it; to put it another way, in the look the painting itself becomes the look, and if every painting ultimately becomes what it paints, it is doubtless always through the look that this happens—by which I mean both through the look from out of which painting emerges *and* through the look that it becomes in the very act of painting it.[2]

Now, this look does not look at any particular object. It is always turned elsewhere, sometimes toward the painter/spectator,[3] at other times toward an indeterminate outside. (Lotto's young man, afflicted as he is by a slight squint, does one thing with the left eye, the other with his right.) At still other times, it is lost or rapt in itself, as we say, infinitely other and the same.[4]

The look of the portrait looks at nothing, and looks at the nothing. As it plunges headlong into the absence of the subject (mine, its own; ours, too, by definition, common and divided), it looks at no object. To look at nothing is, first and foremost, the intimate contradiction of the subject (the contrariness in which an intimacy takes place). Yet the contradiction is resolved or suspended once we understand that the look is ultimately not a relation to the object. What we tend to call "sight" *is* perhaps just such a relation, and in this sense the portrait sees nothing and is not there to be seen. "Sight" belongs to the domain of objects. The look, by contrast, brings the subject to the fore. "To look at" means, first and foremost, *to look out for* or *to look after*, to ward or *warten*, to watch or guard over. To be concerned with or to care for. By looking, I look out for and guard (myself); I am related to the world, not to the object. Only thus can I say that I "am." In seeing, I see, by way of optics; in looking I am myself at stake. I cannot look *without this look looking back at me.*[5] What the portrait presents is always this looking out for oneself—and with it, this: how *the* self looks out for itself because it loses its way. How its being-to-itself takes place only in this outside-itself, before itself, where a face unknown to it looks the world square in the face.

This has nothing to do either with phenomena or with a phenomenology. There is nothing aimed at [*visée*] here. On the contrary, there is an absenting of aim [*la visée*] and, ultimately, of vision. Equally, there is nothing here that would respond to appearance: the look of the portrait never sees anything appear unless it is precisely the nothing, the very thing that does not appear. Nothing rises out of the depths; the ground is there, right on the surface. It does not become surface; rather, like the black cap and cloak of Lotto's young man, like Gumpp's or Pellerin's clothes, it is always the ground becoming face, facing *itself.*

The portrait extracts and exposes the immobile presence, immutable and mute, eternal and instantaneous, of its ground. The ground is a look. Equally, the entire face becomes an eye, as happens in the case of the young man, his face set in dark, dark cloth. It is no longer a question of a particular visual organ; rather, it is a matter of a guarded presence, a presence that watches out both for itself and for the other. All portraits watch out and watch out for themselves; they survey themselves (their preservation or their bearing, their reserve) and look out for themselves (their demise, their passing away, and their abandonment).

But what opens this look and the way in which it looks out for itself is nothing other than the canvas as a whole, all of which can be said to look: the eye, for example, that the lamp lights up in the background of the painting. The painting looks with its entire painterly being [*son être de peinture*].

Every portrait—and so every painting—opens up from its ground to its surface, moving in front of itself, jumping ahead of itself, both in the manner of its encounter and in the manner of its distancing. This look particular to painting doubles the look of the portrait (even though every look is double: one eye on itself, one eye on the other). There are numerous ways in which the look of a particular person can be multiplied or intensified while still diverted or transposed with regard to the painting itself: the lamp in the Lotto, but also the painting hung on the wall or the touch of red on the decoration

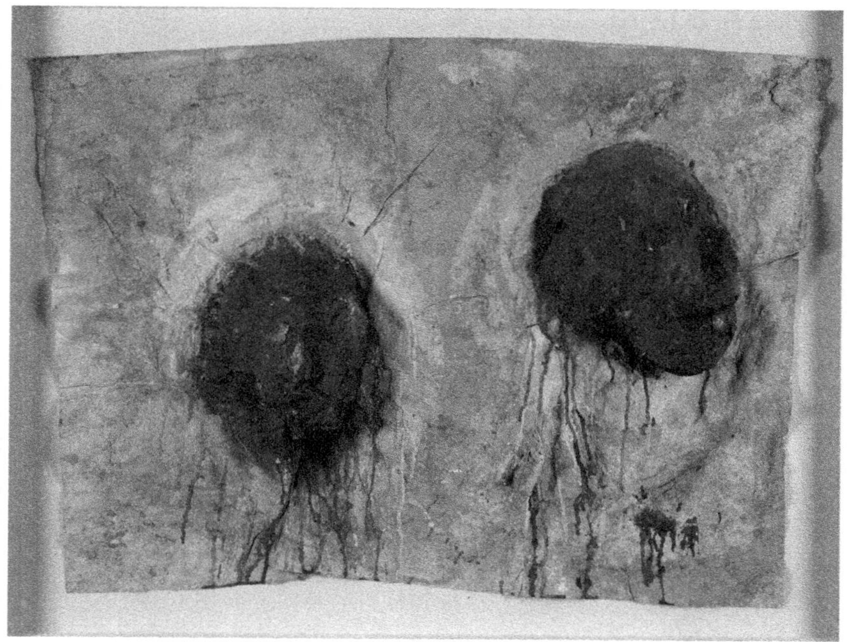

Figure 4

pinned to the jacket in the Matisse portrait of Auguste Pellerin; elsewhere a pearl, a ring, the eye of an animal, a mirror, the tip of a breast, a magnifying glass, a reflection in brass, the red mouth, or the depiction of another drawing, even another painting, in the portrait itself, even the allegorical look of Painting, as in one of Poussin's self-portraits: various ways in which painting is turned into the look of the look, into what looks out for it, its protector, its sighting, and its encounter. Various ways of *drawing the eye—of drawing it to itself outside itself.*

In 1994, Miguel Barceló paints his *Double Portrait* (Figure 4). In doing so, he takes up or highlights a traditional genre of the double or triple portrait that dates back at least to Giorgione and Raphael (then to Rigaud and many others). What immediately leaps out at us, however, is the metamorphosis of the canvas into a close-up on the look, into a sort of unique other of the double portrait in which the two heads become eyes.

Those eyes devour the real portraits that, from the outset, the title alone, as is only right and proper, identifies as being portraits. In each of the dark, round masses[6] we can, albeit only just, discern certain traces or certain evanescent touches of a face—a nose and a mouth rather than eyes—to the point that we can even hazard a guess that the portrait on the right is looking to the right while the one on the left is looking straight ahead. These vestigial faces, however, these two dark masses, are also nothing more than two eyes, even two open pupils, because they show no signs of opening at their center and are themselves the opening of the painting.

Eye masses, a look that is amassed, thrown, torn, even broken, flowing with black blood. This canvas can and should be seen as a look of death, as the death of the look and as death in the look. But it can also and indeed *should*—without any contradiction whatsoever—be seen in the way that the title invites: as the fullness of a double look whose entire ground rises up to the surface, as two subjects together, as their society into which we ourselves sink our eyes because it draws us with them, into the association of looks turned in different directions [*en sens divers*].

Their obscure depth is nothing other than the look overflowing its own surface: The dense color of the two portraits spills from the eyes, spills onto the ground and blends into it. The subject heads into what surrounds it, itself becoming the surround or the surround becoming the subject. But what is a surround? It is what sets up the place for a look to take place, what sets a look in place. It is the convergence [*convenance*][7] of the coming and the presence of the subject, a welcoming and a gathering in order for it to come into the world.

At the same time that the subject wholly completes itself as work—if the work is the one and only place in which a subject is wholly referred back to itself, in which a substance is able to cling to itself, under itself, in the same way that the colored paste clings to the canvas it impregnates—the subject-work does nothing but open onto and overflow a look that is no longer a substance but an opening, no longer a return to itself but an exposition of it.

Wittgenstein writes: "We don't see the human eye as a receiver. . . . When you see the eye, you see something go out from it. You see the blink of an eye [*Blick des Auges*]."[8]

The look, Wittgenstein's *Blick*, is the thing that leaves or takes its leave, the thing of leaving. More precisely, the look is nothing phenomenal; on the contrary, it is the *thing in itself* of a departure from the self through which alone the subject becomes a subject. Far from being a look directed toward an object, the thing in itself of the departure or opening is an opening toward a world. In truth, it is no longer even a look *upon* but a look as a whole, open not *on* but *through* the evidence of the world.

In the look of the portrait, the work's closure in upon itself coincides in a quite blinding (revelatory, luminous) way with an infinite excess over this closure. It is no longer the representation of a subject placed before a world;

instead, it is nothing less than the presentation of a world rising up into its own vision, into its own evidence.

The solution of the subject or the *self* is its dissolution and resolution. The problem of self-relation is exposed and untangled in a look devoid of relation, in a look that looks upon itself only to the extent that it paints itself and thereby departs from itself.

The portrait will have brought into focus the ontological problematic of the subject in the whole extent of its constitutive distension and the entire tension of its ambivalence. On the other hand—presence in itself—closure in the work, the sovereign figure, the glorification of vision and the face; on the other—presence set outside itself—the gesture and the touch of painting, the figure gone astray, the look lost in the rhythm of its own capture. And yet the two sides are, in fact, the two faces of the same canvas; not in the sense of a face to face encounter but in the sense of an internal division of *a single back-to-back face*. Only painting can formulate thus the entire structure and genesis of the subject, *the dark intimacy of the figured and colored surface*, the shadow being brought *into the painting* by the portrait.

Only painting, then, can provide the subject with his or her own words, without either voice or language that could be rendered by discourse, and without, too, this name "subject." What it designates or names is shown here to be a single *trait*: not a self-relation, not a resemblance or a recollection of the self, but the trait of an intimate disunion, the plane of an eclipse of an encounter missed in advance because it turns immediately, with the same stroke, with the same brush stroke, into the spacing of a world with its attraction and its disquiet. "Art" is the fragile name of this other encounter.[9] And isn't a portrait first and foremost an encounter?

It is to this that our contemporary world responds, simultaneously emptying and cutting through the look of the portrait but also (and thus) exacerbating and extending it, opening it out and leading it away from the face (Picasso), leading it toward what lies furthest within the canvas (Giacometti), what torments it (Bacon) or brings it forth, hyperrealized in an acrylic-acid clarity, scrawls on it or smears it, transforming it into a white block, and what becomes thus, ever more vertiginously, a look that plunges headlong into the evasion of the look itself, the look of the painter as well as the look of the other—one plunged into the other, into the protection of the flight itself,[10] meeting in a flash of the *sub* and the *jectum*, of the support and the painting.

Here, the subject is no longer, as is or would seem to be the case with the Cartesian and philosophical model in general, the self-evidence of an interiority held within itself by the suspension of the world. Increasingly, it throws off resemblance and recollection understood in terms of humanism, intentionality, and representation (from which, however, as we know, painting will continually struggle to free itself). By hollowing out the look, however, by emptying it or aggravating it at the same time as it digs deep, turning its eyes in on itself, painting intensifies this same look, even to the extent of aggravating it if need be. This is how it portrays beyond the portrait itself.

In a sense, it never ceases do to what Hegel said that it did when he spoke of the *life of Spirit*, and in this regard all portrait painters are Hegelian (as they were long before Hegel), right up to the demolition of the portrait itself. The whole point is to know how the "life of Spirit" is faced and defaced, how the return to self loses itself in its look.

To be lost in a look; isn't this what we mean by painting? But drawn thus outside of itself in the *act of its being painted*, the look becomes the evidence of a world that is exposed less before me as a spectacle than *through* me as a force that opens my eyes in the eyes of the painting, in the opening out and bedazzlement that painting certainly does not represent but that it *is* or that it *paints*, because in what we call "art," *to paint* or *to portray* means nothing less than the sense or meaning of *being* and so of being in the world. The painted look plunges into this *in*.

—*Translated by Simon Sparks*

The Other Portrait

What is the situation today with the artistic genre or form of the portrait? In one sense, this question involves the past or traditional character of the portrait in the history of Western art—and consequently, the question of a becoming with its transformations, its ruptures, its motives, and its surprises. At the same time, it also involves the particular character of the portrait inasmuch as it constitutes a focal point for "figuration" in general—therefore, for mimesis—and a type of production whose belonging to art is not straightforward because the portrait has aims and uses that are in principle independent of whatever artistic statement it might also be making.

With the portrait—with its modes, its manners, its eclipses, and its ruins—what is being played out is the fate of the figure in general: the fate of representation, of fiction, therefore of presence and of truth; of the face, of presence and absence; of the other, its proximity and its distance. In the portrait, what is being distinctly retraced, withdrawn, and replayed right before our eyes is the very possibility of our being present.

L'altro ritratto

L'altro ritratto: This expression, formulated in Italian, was initially proposed as a theme for an art exhibit.[1] Two meanings of the phrase immediately arise: On the one hand, "the other portrait" suggests a portrait different from the one we know, the one we think we have passably identified in terms of a notion or idea of "portrait"; on the other hand, and according to the proper resources of Italian, "the other withdrawn [*retiré*]" suggests the other as the other of the same (or the proper, or the self) considered in terms of a withdrawal—a retreat, a recoil, indeed, a disappearance—that would itself be an effect or property of the portrait.

This expression therefore presents two demands: one is to consider the difference or differences proper to the contemporary portrait, provided that it is possible to risk claiming a sort of defining feature; the other is to consider the withdrawal of the other in its very (re)presentation in the portrait. The two demands are connected, if the contemporary portrait places the accent—many sorts of accent—on the flight or strangeness of the person of whom the portrait is made.

According to its ordinary meaning, the "portrait" designates the representation of a person, specifically his or her face. This meaning is a specialization of a larger one: of drawing, representation in general, figuration, indeed inscription or engraving (as with the "letter portraits" engraved on the swords of Chrétien de Troyes). The prefix *por* (originally, *pour*) marks an intensification: the line, the outline is applied or carried forth and its intensity sends it in the direction of a substitution of the drawing for the thing drawn. The "pourtraict" or "portrait" also signified the drawing of the forms of a building to be constructed, or indeed the description of a state of things or of a notion (for example, health).[2] In current French, it is still possible to speak of the portrait of a situation, of a region, of an activity, etc. ("tableau" or "portrayal" are also used in this way—for example, in "the portrayal of urban customs").

The Italian language has retained the composition of the Latin *trahere* or *traciare*, with the added prefix *re* marking the extraction of the trait, the action of pulling it out of the model in order to reproduce it. At the same time as it signifies "portrait," *ritratto* also designates "retreat," "retraction," or "withdrawal"—a meaning rediscovered in the French *retraite*. (By contrast, in certain regions of France the verb *retraire* used to mean "resemble.") As is the case with "portrait," *ritratto* also had the non-specialized meaning of "representation."

Between the *portrait* and the *ritratto* an intriguing semantic complexity develops.[3] On the one hand, the figuration of the human face (or the representation of a whole body) incorporates the general value of figuration—just as, incidentally, *figure* and *figura* can, in French and Italian respectively, incorporate the general value of the outlined contour, of the form given shape, into the human figure: In certain contexts, "figure" practically becomes a synonym for "face," although in other contexts, it tends in the direction of the "geometrical figure." The face is valued for the excellence of its look (it is a matter of seeing the "seer"), its representation, and its image (a good image must in some way stare at us . . .).

On the other hand, two movements intersect: One is an intensity that puts forth and impresses the features, and the other is a disengagement or excision that draws the features to itself in order to express them. The one moves toward a putting-into-presence, right up to the point of replacing the model with the image ("You'd half expect it to speak"); the other moves toward reproduction and likeness, allowing for a comparison of the image to the model ("It's well and truly him!"). At the limit, one could say that the logic of *mimesis*, such as it gets concentrated in the portrait, is always suspended—or stretched—between the one extreme of pure presence (one that abolishes *mimesis*) and the other extreme of similarity (where *mimesis* underscores the absence of the model, indeed, its disappearance).

This entire intricacy of values and valences comes up again in the complexity surrounding the notion of *representation*: Imitative presentation, which draws from or borrows the qualities of the original in order to reproduce them, mingles with the gesture of a presentation to a spectator whose attention is drawn (such is the old meaning of the expression "faire des représentations"), to which we could also add the politico-juridical meaning according to which a *representative* (for example, a deputy) is mandated by an agent. The portrait combines precisely these three functions: It reproduces, it makes an appeal, and it is founded in power. So, the portrait of a sovereign or master depicts, evokes, and exercises his or her authority (or some aspect of it).

As a result, the *portrait/ritratto* carries the problematic of representation or figure to incandescence: The exteriority of a showing vies with the intimacy of a capture performed on what is most proper. In the portrait, expressing outward and plunging inward are opposing and, at the same time, complementary. That is why one can speak of the portrait, to use Jean-Christophe Bailly's phrase, as the "absolute of the image."[4]

Such are the initial stakes of what we have named *l'altro ritratto*: In the portrait, in *its* portrait—in its "proper" portrait (an expression that could not be more ambiguous)—the other withdraws. The other withdraws in showing itself; it makes a retreat within its very expression. The portrayed other is also the withdrawn other. Consequently, the other who is recognized—if resemblance is the same as recognition—is also the other who becomes more unknown than before this recognition. He is more unknown because he is withdrawn in his alterity. But this retreat reveals the mystery of this alterity: It does not unveil the mystery but rather reveals that it is a matter of a mystery—and that there is no question of dispelling it.

—|—

At this point, another knot of signification arises: On the one hand, thinking about the portrait in terms of resemblance involves the copy's similarity to the model, but only to the extent that the model *resembles himself or herself*, that is, is indeed "himself" or "herself." It sometimes happens that, as one says, someone "doesn't seem like themselves" (or indeed we also say of a gesture or an action that "that's not like him"). On the other hand, thinking about the portrait in terms of substitution implies, at least at the extreme, the absence of the model and therefore his or her virtual death. The portrait is therefore linked to the *imago*, the wax bust of an ancestor, whose preparation, possession, and display constituted a privilege of the Roman patriciate.

Nevertheless, actual death is not the only horizon of absence: The portrait implies an essential absence that is contemporaneous with the living presence of its model. There are countless reflections inspired by this absenting as an integral part of the image, particularly since the invention of photography. If the most dramatic character of absence offered by the portrait has to do with its evocation of death—past or future—its most disquieting character is found still elsewhere: in the possibility that the absence at issue is not only the absence of the model for the spectator of the portrait, but the absence of the model from him- or herself.

How is the *self* the same as itself? The portrait opens onto the confusion of this questioning, which is raised in conjunction with the shock of death when, in an exemplary manner in the history of art, religion, and the portrait, portraits of the deceased were attached to the mummies of Fayoum (a practice still carried on today when photographs are placed on tombs or in front of urns).[5] We know that the deceased person no longer has this face that was, however, once his or her own: We therefore no longer really know what "his or her own" means.

The sameness of self, or ipseity, implies not only a strict identity but also its exclusivity and its authenticity: "Oneself" appeals to a personality, an autonomy, and an un-substitutability. How then to figure or give form to a substitution that is acceptable and consistent with the un-substitutable?

At this point, the quite brutal possibility suggests itself that the true likeness of an *ipse* with it-*self* can only be given by its dead face, and its only portrait by its death mask.[6] But the suspicion immediately follows from this that, in some way, every portrait functions like a death mask: It converts the absence of the person who is present into the presence of the person who is absent. There is the presence of a mask here, more than there is a masked presence; that is, at issue here is a presence that recovers nothing and expresses nothing but the hollow of its entire volume. A parallel demonstration is *ipso facto* given an imposing weight: It warns the spectator of the opening in himself of a similar absence.

The other withdraws into the abyss of its portrait—and it is in me that the echo of this retreat resonates.

However the painter, the photographer, or the sculptor also works at pulling the other back from this abyss. But in this case it is a matter of an operation that is entirely different from that of a copy or a cast. The death mask shows nothing more than the look of a dead face—that is, a face that has become a stranger to itself. In certain respects, this look is instructive regarding the look of death—if we disregard the various techniques that must be used to make the cast both possible and acceptable—but it intensifies the enigma of the identity to self.

For all that though, the portrait does not produce a resolution to this enigma. Insofar as it functions as a death mask, it is itself only the cast of the enigma as such. But insofar as it activates the double process of the "expression" and "im-pression" of "features" (lines, traces, looks, models, styles, pallor and tinges, tensions, attentions, hesitations, and so on), it elaborates, gives shape to, and represents—that is, it fabricates [*il fictionne*]—what we might be tempted to call an "interpretation" of the person portrayed, provided that we distinguish this thinking of "interpretation" from the common usage of the word—that is, as a biased perspective on what is originally given. For there is no pure and simple "original given" here because the *ipse* "in itself" is not given and can only be the infinitely absent (either dead or *dreamed up*).

To the contrary, the interpretation in question here should be understood in terms of the musical interpretation of a score, the reading of which alone would not actually make us hear tones, colors, or vibrations. In this sense, the interpretation as a putting-into-play and as a putting to work of a meaning that does not pre-exist it—or else that only pre-exists as a virtuality that calls for and awaits its actuality—constitutes a formal property of every artistic gesture: What is to be interpreted is not given, is neither present before the interpretation nor is it outside of it. Everything that has to do with "art" has to do with an invention of meaning that is not completed or enclosed in the executed form, in the accomplished work. For the work essentially opens onto the reengagement, onto the revival of its invention.

The operation to which the portrait is given over can be designated as a characterization. *Character* first designates (in Greek) an imprint, a distinctive mark printed onto an object—in particular onto a piece of money, where we actually find the first portraits of sovereigns—to mark an outline or else a profile from the most appropriate side.[1] Character is discriminating, appropriate, singular, remarkable, and to put it frankly . . . original. In this way, characterization brings about an original configuration by which a singular attribute is distinguished. It is in this sense that "character" indicates an individual mark at the interior of a writing, as well as a temperament or personality in its particular relief.

It is precisely in this way that Machiavelli could compose *ritratti* that are not descriptions properly speaking, but are rather more like collections of observations and reflections drawn from legations and other missions of the High Chancellor of Florence. They bear all the marks of selection, judgment, and the interests of their author, for whom it is not a question of "representing" but of deepening the reflection by characterizing the experiences for the benefit of an eye focused squarely on the fate of cities and governments.

Every portrait consists of a characterization, an observation that is selective, reflexive, and questioning. This characterization does not attempt to restore a character but rather, configures one: not *the* supposedly "true" or "authentic" character of what is represented, but *a* character such that it is marked and distinguished *for itself*, producing its sameness, its propriety, its singularity *in itself*, in this "in-itself" of the portrait or as this in-itself, and not within a supposed "subject in itself." Many characterizations, interpretations, portraits of this subject are possible and every time it exhibits a new character, a new variation, nuance, or tonality at the bottom of which the "in-itself," or what we could call the "absolute character" of the subject, withdraws.

Therefore, each characterization characterizes it as *such*—according to the unique quality of such a portrait—and, at the same time, as *other*. Each portrait traces from its singular feature the sameness according to *such* a mode and according to the inexhaustible alterity of its model.

—+—

But the "subject" has a history: It has not always existed, or at least it has not always been thought as such, *it has not always thought itself as such*, and not always consistently. If the portrait is "rooted in the subject," as Schefer puts it in the phrase used as the epigram for this book, we need to rehearse the modalities of this rootedness along the course of history.

It is in accordance with this history that the concept of model itself vacillates in proportion to this mingling of sameness and alterity, that is, in proportion to the distance from itself to which the portrait bears witness. In the very place of this gap, in the interval of self to self, in the difference of the self and consequently in its infinite presence-to-self that hollows out an absence amenable both to its arrival and to its departure—that is, to the expression of its figure on its un-figurable ground—the portrait/*ritratto* consists of a fiction [*une fiction*] that constitutes the truth of the self (we must remember that "fiction" and "figure" share the same origin and almost the same meaning).

The portrait is a fiction—that is, it is a *figuration* not in the sense of mimetic representation of a figure but in the much stronger and more active sense of the creation of a figure, of modeling (*fingo, fictum*), and of a mise-en-scène of a "figure" in the sense of "personage" or "role" and also of "emblem," "expression," or of "remarkable form" (in all the senses of the "representative" indicated previously). Nevertheless, the figure proposed by the portrait has nothing to represent or put into play other than itself. When it is a question of an illustrious person, the portrait must, of course, place value on the grandeur of the person's function (their majesty, their power, their notoriety) but it can devote itself exclusively to this end only by refraining from portraying the private person. However, tremors of intimacy demand to be figured or portrayed, too, just as much as public glory does. Fame or glory demands as much because by definition, it participates in a projection and a symbolization, and privacy does so because it largely shies away from the exteriority of form and exposition. The two seem to push up against one another yet each calls upon the other, in short, to support it: Privacy wants to be pointed out or recognized in order to be respected and fame wants people to imagine that it is inhabited by a secret.

The Eye

In one way or another though, the portrait is in some sense aimed at a distant and unattainable reality, one in relation to which it is measured and thought. The portrait is turned toward the recoil, removal, or withdrawal of an alterity and it is only exposed to our gazes in order to show us how it is exposed to this alterity. More precisely, the alterity of its "subject"—in the pictorial sense, its figure, as well as in the ontological sense, the ipseity within the figure—opens the retreat and carries away the withdrawal, the interminable sliding toward a depth whose thin surface in two dimensions indicates that it is unfathomable.

This unfathomable is what the portrait penetrates and exposes. "Making the invisible visible" is often thought to be a modern formulation. But Paul Klee's well-known formulation—"*Kunst gibt nicht das Sichtbare wieder, sondern Kunst macht sichtbar*" ("Art does not reproduce the visible; rather, it makes visible")—is only properly modern to the extent that in 1920, he felt it necessary to distance himself once again from the non-artistic (and indeed, disastrous for how the public thinks of art) influence of imitation, of "rendering," of the "natural," and of the "similar." What Klee was trying to affirm has never been ignored by artists. One could not even so much as look at images that have survived from the Paleolithic era if, through them, we did not have access to an immediate understanding of the following: Those who painted them were seeking to make something visible that remained absent from the entire spectacle offered to perception.

That which is most invisible to perception is not darkness—for after all, we do see darkness, even if we see nothing in it. What is most invisible is rather vision itself, which by definition cannot look back on itself. It could be that the heart of the problematic of self-relation, of presence to self and in itself, is to be found in the relation of the look to itself. More than any other sense, vision escapes from outside and moves away from its place of operation whereas hearing, touch, taste, and smell all intermingle their "outside" with their "inside" and function entirely within a chiasm or resonance of the one and the other. The eye is as if lost for vision because it is projected in it and as if expelled in it; the eye cannot see itself and yet what it wants to see is vision, *its* vision.

Perhaps the portrait must be considered in terms of the way the look returns to itself, not in the mode of a reflection but in that of a penetration into itself that makes more than its appearance visible: This very invisibility from which it looks, its *macula*, its blind spot—that makes of its art a blind *task*, a labor that gropes around in the dark abyss of the "self" or the "*ipse.*" The portrait would be based less on the frontal vision—the painter or photographer facing the model—than on this improbable vision that Descartes practiced when he looked from the back of a sliced cow's eye, hoping to see how the eye sees.[1] Conversely, the look of a portrait is also often said to be the most penetrating—and the most penetrated—of looks, as well as being what Baudelaire discerns when he writes the following:

> When I study, in the gaslight which colors it,
> Your pale forehead, embellished with a morbid charm,
> Where the torches of evening kindle a dawn,
> And your eyes alluring as a portrait's,[2] . . .

—┼—

The logic we are pursuing here would lead us to say that all visual art is "portrait," at least in principle. Perhaps it is not actually necessary to refute this conclusion. It could very well be that the heart of visual art ("visual" as well as, or even more so, "visionary" . . .) is constituted by a double authority: On the one hand, the active intervention into the visible, that is, the formal theme, the wavy or broken line, the rhythmic mark, the surge of the line and the burst of the spot, and on the other hand, the eye experiencing itself in the movement or the pushing that pulls the line, that accentuates the planes and the relations, that casts the smudge or bleeds it. The eye, withdrawing in some way from the views projected in front of it, palpating within itself the texture and the energy of its seeing—just as a portrait never ceases to withdraw into itself the view that it offers to whoever looks at it, a view that in the end belongs only to the portrait, to the darkness at the base of its eyes, and the gesture of the portraitist is being pulled toward this darkness.

Visageity

If it is not always, or even primarily, a matter of the portrait in the sense in which we distinguish it from other kinds of representation—landscapes, scenes, objects, non-mimetic forms—it could well be that the portrait involves an element, a valence, or an urge that takes place in every type of visual proposition: the visibility of visuality and through it, a "visageity" that one could also discern in a landscape or a still-life. To content ourselves with just one formulation of this important and already well-worked theme, we will cite Jean-Louis Schefer: "The experience of seeing poses the question of sense in a complex way, primarily in that the 'thing' seen or contemplated is only visible by a kind of activity that is going on within it."[1]

So in effect we can look at the activity—the look—of a landscape by Corot (Figure 5). But let's remain with the portrait "properly" speaking, even though we could venture the claim that all painting (drawing, photography . . .) is a "metaphor" of the portrait.

That the portrait is strongly associated with the visage (incidentally, the latter word used to have the same meaning as the former: A *visage* was a *portrait* before being a *face*) not only means that the portrait shows the side [*la face*] of the person that is most visibly individualizing and expressive, but also that this side is the one upon which the look appears. The face [*le visage*] makes visible the vision that, strictly speaking, itself remains invisible, for the eye "itself" is not yet vision.

Although cave painting offers only a very limited number of faces, it should nonetheless be emphasized that there are many looks to be seen on the animal heads, those of stags, bison, horses, lions, and others (Figure 6).

The fact that there are no people represented makes these looks all the more important. We might speculate on the extent to which they are "fixed" by those who paint them: The painter "fixes" them in two senses of the word, visual (by observing them) and pictorial (by painting them)—and in so doing,

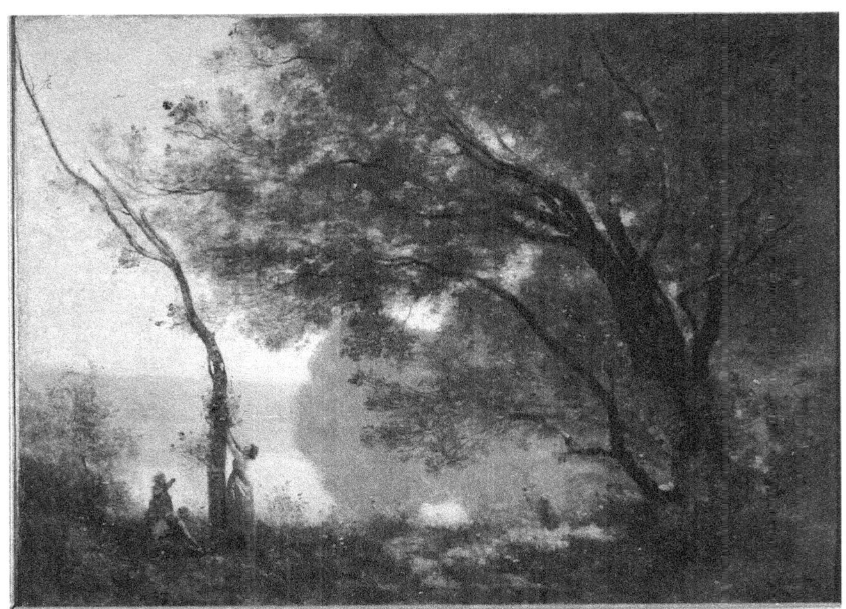

Figure 5

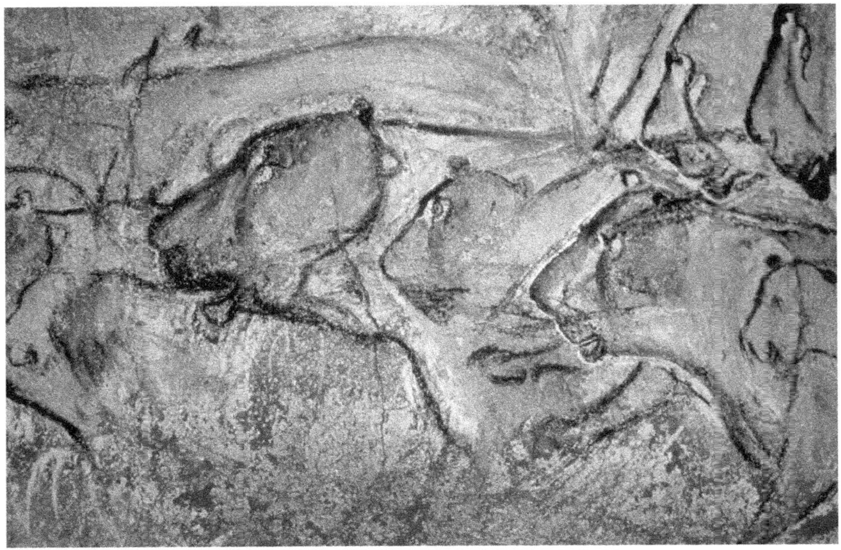

Figure 6

he or she makes the power of vision itself arrive before his or her very eyes, in what is visible, along with what that vision itself retains of tension, traction, attraction, and contraction toward an outside. That way, a "within" is revealed, that is, not an "interior" entity or region but the totality of a projected body toward an elsewhere (prey, obstacle, menace . . .). This body is thus revealed as something other than a simple presence positioned here or there: It is shown to be the opening of a place, orientation, and aim, a relation to something and to other bodies in the world.

Mimesis

A portrait presents above all the tension of a relation, but not a relation to "someone" else. To the contrary, a relation between two characters is not necessarily a "double portrait" but could just as well be offering up a scene or narrative, whereas the portrait does not tell a story but arrests every kind of speech, narration, or declaration in order to sustain an almost exclusive relation to itself. At the same time, the portrait's self-relation constitutes the entire substance of the relation to the spectator, who is presented with someone as a "self" and not as an interlocutor—except perhaps as a silent interlocutor of itself. To put it in these terms: I am presented with a "me" (or an "I") and therefore with another me and/or the "me" of another ...

When it is a question of a "double portrait," the scene that is initiated or suggested between the characters is at the same time suspended, held back in favor of two separate presentations, each of which is referring to itself and between which it is not even clear that a relation exists apart from the fact that they are both being exposed to our look.

Such is the case with Giorgione's *Double Portrait* from 1502 (Figure 7), assuming it is indeed a question of a "double portrait" as the canonical title suggests, and not of an isolated moment within a storyline that we may know nothing about. But this comes down to insisting on the fact that a portrait must be presented as such and judged consequently, although it can always be an image taken out of context and separated from a chain of actions. There are, of course, portraits placed within crowd scenes (the well-known self-portraits of Raphaël and Dürer, among many others). The so-called "autonomous" portrait—presumed valuable solely as a portrait—is at its core only a limit-concept, tied to a thinking of the "subject" that we are going to have to discuss.

It is in this respect that the portrait shows itself as an excellent resemblance: Never will it be said that a landscape or a still-life "resembles" with

Figure 7

the same force and concern used in reference to how a portrait "resembles." It seems obvious to us that the likeness of an apple or a tree matters little in comparison with the likeness of a face, although if one is committed to the exactness of a reproduction in accordance with a defined vision, there is no reason to judge things in this way.

Better still: The portrait in its essence seems to be contemporaneous with the Greek invention of *mimesis*. Without doubt, it is not exactly present in classical Greece in the manner—which we gladly call "realist"—of the Roman

portrait. Aside from indirect witnesses to certain portraits depicting supposedly historical figures, the human figure still conforms to canons as opposed
to singular identities. Nevertheless, the Greek legend involving the famous
fiancé of Butade's daughter initiates painting through the silhouette of a
person, and what Plato calls "knowledgeable *mimesis*," that is, that which
imitates wisely, is characterized through the reproduction of "the person or
voice" of Socrates.[1]

However, what is essential here is not concerned with "realism" as soon
as it is well and truly a matter of the human face and the human body[2] in
place of the archetypal and hierophantic figures (at times half-animal, half-
human) that seem to us to have come before the properly mimetic age of the
West.[3] What is essential to *mimesis* does not involve the reproduction of forms
that are exactly identifiable: It holds to the fact of seeking out, in man and in
the human world, a witness to the enigma (mystery, divinity, force, sacrality)
that other cultures are going to look for in typified human forms (through
a hieratism or a symbolism), be they animal, vegetal, mineral, or "abstract"
(motifs that are geometric, wavy, etc., and all no less "typified").

Put otherwise, *mimesis* cannot simply be understood as an eradication of
the hierophantic dimension: Rather, this dimension enters into a metamorphosis of the act we call "artistic." To be sure, this act has always possessed
a properly "aesthetic" dimension. But even when the aesthetic seems to
saturate the artistic gesture entirely (as it does in our modernity), its significance or its stakes are still not simply aesthetic. It is indeed exactly for
this reason that the word "art"—a term whose actual usage is less than two
centuries old—endlessly renews the challenge of its meaning and not only as
a semantic disquiet but also as a challenge which is henceforth co-substantial
with the very practices that it is supposed to designate.

Let us risk an overly simplistic formulation. *Mimesis* does not "figure" the
gods "under the guise of human appearances": It brings forth divine presence
in an appearing that is the appearance of man, just as much as *politeia* makes
the communal order appear within the autonomy of the human city and
just as much as *logos*, far from simply dethroning *mythos*, seeks to make the
speech of origins resonate in an autonomous, recognizable, and human mode.

As with politics and logic, *mimesis* bears within it the premise of autonomy.
In this sense, every portrait—including, as we suggested previously, every representation—is a *self-portrait*. This well-known assertion is ordinarily understood in a reductively psychological way, related to a type of narcissism thought
to be constitutive of the artistic gesture (or of every production of form). But
in truth, if representation always advances the three related values identified
earlier—depicting, appealing, being a representative—then we must also take

into consideration what, for each of these three functions, would have to be called *autotelic*, a finality situated in the *auto*, or the oneself.

Autos, or self, is what survives after the gods—that is, the others—have withdrawn and no longer set the standard (other than formally or conventionally), once their *mythos* is declared a "fiction." *Autos* survives precisely at the site and in the movement of this retreat. It takes on the full force of this retreat as well as its whole enigma: It is from the self, and no longer from others, that language must speak, the city must be organized, and the figure must be presented. From the self *as other*.

Withdrawn Presence

This is doubtless one way of understanding the claim made by Pessoa that the divinity of the Greek gods consists in their statues. These statues do not represent divinity but present it; they themselves are that divinity. For Pessoa, that could mean that there is nothing divine beyond this beautiful appearance, or more accurately, nothing beyond this beautiful appearing, which is not a phenomenon grounded in a thing "in itself" but, within the tautology of its form, is itself all there is of the divine. For us, this will mean a little more: The divine appears in the resemblance of the human form to itself.

Or at least, let us hope that the divine appears in this autonomous resemblance, not—to be very clear—in a figure meant to give an analogical or allegorical representation, an evocation, or an "idea" of the mysterious identity of god, but in an entirely different manner: in a figure that shows itself to be the appearing of a self-relation in which the divine resides.

To substantiate this claim, we must take a brief detour through a philosophical consideration that might seem extrinsic to art but will nonetheless offer us the chance to understand how, with *mimesis*, the first form arises of what will finally become "art" in terms of a specific category. It is a matter of what we have become accustomed to calling the *subject*. This term first signified the same thing as *substance*: that which is set under and has nothing else below it (in a non-technical manner, we can think of "essence," "foundation," or "nature" as equivalents). But *subject* was belatedly specialized to designate what we understand to be the "subject" of a consciousness, an identity, a personality (and also a "subject of law"): the non-substitutable unity of a "being self" such that it does not depend on anything else (in the same way that "substance" is itself supported by nothing).

That substance becomes subject signifies—as is shown in an explosive manner by the Hegelian movement of the "experience of consciousness"— that what is set below, what is *supposed* or *presupposed* of an identity in the form of *ego*, is not a simple thing but is already, always already in itself a relation, the relation-to-self that is the very meaning of "self," its nature and its structure.

The *subject* only comes about within a particular culture: when the authorities of judgment, guilt, law, or that of the political decision are no longer considered as given by means of an order that precedes the persons involved (individual or collective) but by means of a "self" that judges, acts, and decides *for itself*. This culture is that by means of which the classical Greek world breaks away from earlier worlds—imperial, rural, theocratic.

The subject is what it is *by itself* and *as itself*. Before it comes to occupy the place assigned to it by social, religious, or ethnic orders, its truth resides in its "sameness." Of course, this disengagement of the subject from these orders occurs gradually, like all profound transformations. It has its first highpoint with Judeo-Christianity and a second quite a bit later with humanism. What should be of interest here involves the fact that *the essence of "itself" demands that its identity, and therefore its identification, proceeds from its sameness.* It is no longer a question of "someone" being identified through his genealogy, group, totem, or function but on the contrary, he must be recognized through himself and through others insofar as those others are the same as him.

It is clear how this process would immediately engage the possibility of the portrait: The *same* is inherent in the *self*; it is the inherence in which the *self* consists and which implies relation, return of the self to self, therefore *sameness* in which its own alterity inheres. The fact that the "same" is always recognizable from the outside[1] of course belongs to the banal experience of perception. But that this recognition also involves the recognition of a fundamental sameness of this other that I recognize as "him- or herself," therein lies precisely what is symptomatic of the first emergence of the subject, or if you prefer, the possibility of the subject.

The reason Aristotle gives for the delight men take in *mimesis*[2] only has meaning in this context: He says that we derive pleasure from saying "It's truly him!"—for this pleasure only takes on its full intensity and thus only warrants an argument when what I identify in a portrait is the "same," not just in this single appearance but in itself, in the invisible sameness that *mimesis* must therefore make visible—and indeed make visible insofar as it gives way.

Of course, Aristotle's formulation applies to every kind of representation (including, as he specifies, the imitations of things that are repellant from a naturalist viewpoint). Indeed, Aristotle is not making any specific claim about the portrait; he is talking about any representation of an object. But his claims only take on their full significance by means of the portrait and the visibility of an invisible sameness, or identity. It should also probably be understood that, starting from the open situation that is related to the sameness-to-self, every representation becomes susceptible to functioning as a representation *of a self* to another *self.* The paintings of a helmet, a horse, or a piece of fruit can be endowed with a kind of "being-subject": In effect, that is where I recognize my own faculty of recognition, my own way of relating to myself in the act of representation, and above all, that is where I discern, along with the thing seen, the way in which my look is moved in this vision. It is, incidentally, only by beginning there that the very idea of "representation," such as it will be elaborated much later, becomes possible.[3] The legitimacy of the distinction between "imitation" (copy, reproduction) and *mimesis* also proceeds from there, concerning which contemporary thought needed to recover the Greek word to distinguish it from a simple reiteration of the identical.[4]

Accordingly, the portrait not only consists of the excellence of an imitation: It is an imitation of what imitates itself or expresses itself in its body and particularly in its face. The portrait represents this representation-of-self or this representation-to-self that makes up the "self." Put otherwise, it represents the representation of an un-representable: My sameness is not a figure that could be externalized in an image but at the same time, the image of my figure carries the return of the non-figure that I "myself" am. The portrait goes hand-in-hand with the invention of an "interiority" that becomes the "object" of *mimesis*, and that becomes that object in such a way that this interiority will end up being sought in all *mimesis*, be it in a landscape or an inanimate object.

Finally, this un-representable interiority becomes such—both "within" and yet "beyond imitation"—because in being recognized, this interiority is recognized beyond the capture of every grasp that would like to give it a shape, by fixing features and colors. What is beyond capture is what, for want of a better alternative, we name the divine, or rather that for which 'the gods" gave shape (and sometimes still do) to a figure charged with representing an alterity that is beyond reach. With the mutation of mimesis, this figure (which was able to adopt the look of an animal, a plant, or a rock) is taken into the human body and the human face. It gives these new features of the human to the alterity and strangeness—indeed, to the monstrosity, the miracle, or the abyss—that had formerly adorned so many different figures. The figuration of the "without face" becomes the face of the "without figure":[5] the same itself, the "self" such that it infinitely exceeds itself. Augustine gives the most complete formulation of this when, in addressing himself to his God, he says: "More inward than my most inward part and higher than the highest element within me."[6]

From then on, a new dimension will open up: The representation of this god will be deemed impossible and its attempt forbidden as the blasphemy known as "idolatry." The idol (in Greek *eidolon,* or little image) is an image insofar as it is taken to be the presence of God. For, the god of Augustine inherits the god of Moses—that is, the god whose presence remains withdrawn from all (re)presentation, and this god is also the one who makes man in his own image. The man of this god thus conforms to the essential withdrawal of his own figure.

Whereas the idol is the image wherein God appears, the portrait could be defined as the image that is given for the withdrawal of what it is the image of—moreover, in a manner consistent with the first sense of *imago* that is the mask of a dead ancestor. The portrait will be tied to death—past or future—of the one whom it represents and it is entirely possible to say that, in the portrait of the West, "God is dead" *avant la lettre*, that is, that God has lost the signs of a presence standing alongside, overseeing, or else clashing with that of men. The mystery is henceforth in man; it is the identity of the other to man within man, and the identity of this other that man is shown to be or is suspected of being: It is on this theme that the singular adventure of Western art begins.

Ipseity

The birth of the portrait[1] therefore takes place under a double constraint: The face of a person, a particular person, must be represented, *and* he or she must be represented according to the sameness of "self" of which he or she is the witness, the expression, in sum the revelation, and indeed also the un-representability. The first exigency moves in the direction of what we call "realism;" the second in the direction of the in-figurable *self* that, it must be clarified, is proper to each and yet at the same time common to all.

In this deeply conflictual or contradictory way, a double movement is released from the first moments of *mimesis* toward idealization and the canon of beauty (the Greek legend of a portrait of a woman composed from many real women) on the one side and, on the other, the imitation of real figures that do not at all conform to that canon. Thus the portrait of an athlete represents a body that itself already conforms to a certain ideal of grace and power (Figure 8), while the image of a grotesque satyr can adorn a wine vessel (Figure 9).

The Roman portrait, famous for its realism, will follow several centuries later (see Figure 10 for a bust of Maximian from the third century).

From there, an ambivalence arises that accompanied the portrait for a long time, from the Renaissance up to the nineteenth century: As a "realistic" representation, that is, identifiable in the sense of reproducing an appearance, the portrait could be construed as a mechanical activity (in the sense of the "mechanical arts" as distinct from the "liberal arts") that does not fall within the category of great painting. Titian, for example, could declare that he was making portraits because he needed money, in spite of the dishonorable character of the practice. In another sense, a realistic portrait could displease a person who sought to present a flattering image of him- or herself. One could write an entire history of the degrees of realism used in portraits of princes and other members of the upper classes, as well as of the flattering embellishments done in those works.

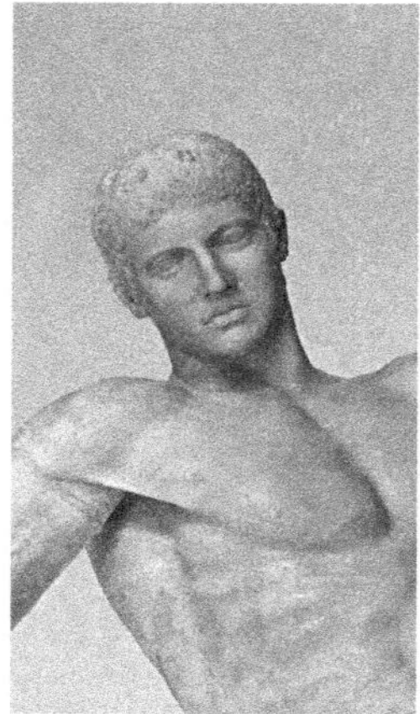

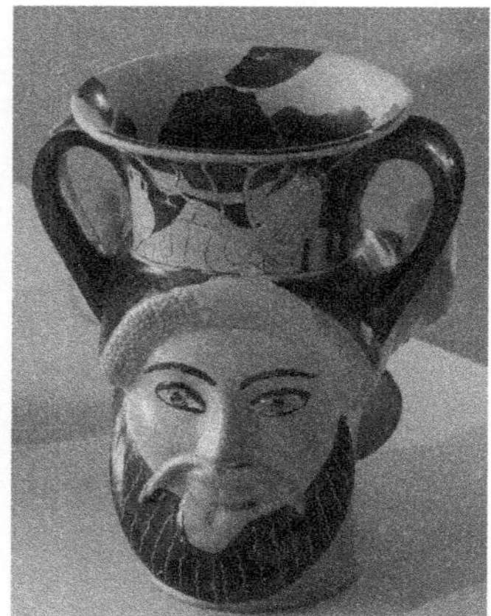

Figure 8   Figure 9

But at the same time, Titian's portraits or else those by Lotto (among many others) bear witness to the presence of a *mimesis* that is attentive to "sameness" or better, to "ipseity" as the real intention of the painter, an ipseity that is itself seemingly unfathomable, as with the young man by Lorenzo Lotto (see Figure 3 in "Recall" from The Look of the Portrait). As we look at such a painting, the everyday understanding of the portrait becomes confused: Is it a matter here of representing someone, of making a kind of allegory of thinking, memory, or melancholy, or is it a matter of presenting an attractive picture? Lotto's work is rich in a more or less esoteric symbolism, but many other portraits can give rise to similar questions. One need only think of the Mona Lisa. Better still: It is always possible to ask whether the characters in a group or even a crowd scene are not also portraits (all of them, or even just a few of them) in the same way that, when we have no means of identifying the person, nothing guarantees that a portrait (as is the case with the portrait by Lotto) is not of a made-up person.

Derrida has noted[2] that nothing guarantees that a self-portrait is actually one, except through some kind of confirmation that is external to the painting. Minor details aside, this is also true of the portrait as soon as one has no means of identification at one's disposal. The question becomes even more explicit in the case of unusual portraits like Ribera's, of a bearded woman carrying an infant: The gossip of the time attests to her existence, but she could just as well have emerged from the imagination of the painter (Figure 11).

When it comes right down to it, the general character of the painting, its somber or luminous atmosphere, gives every portrait its overall tone—a

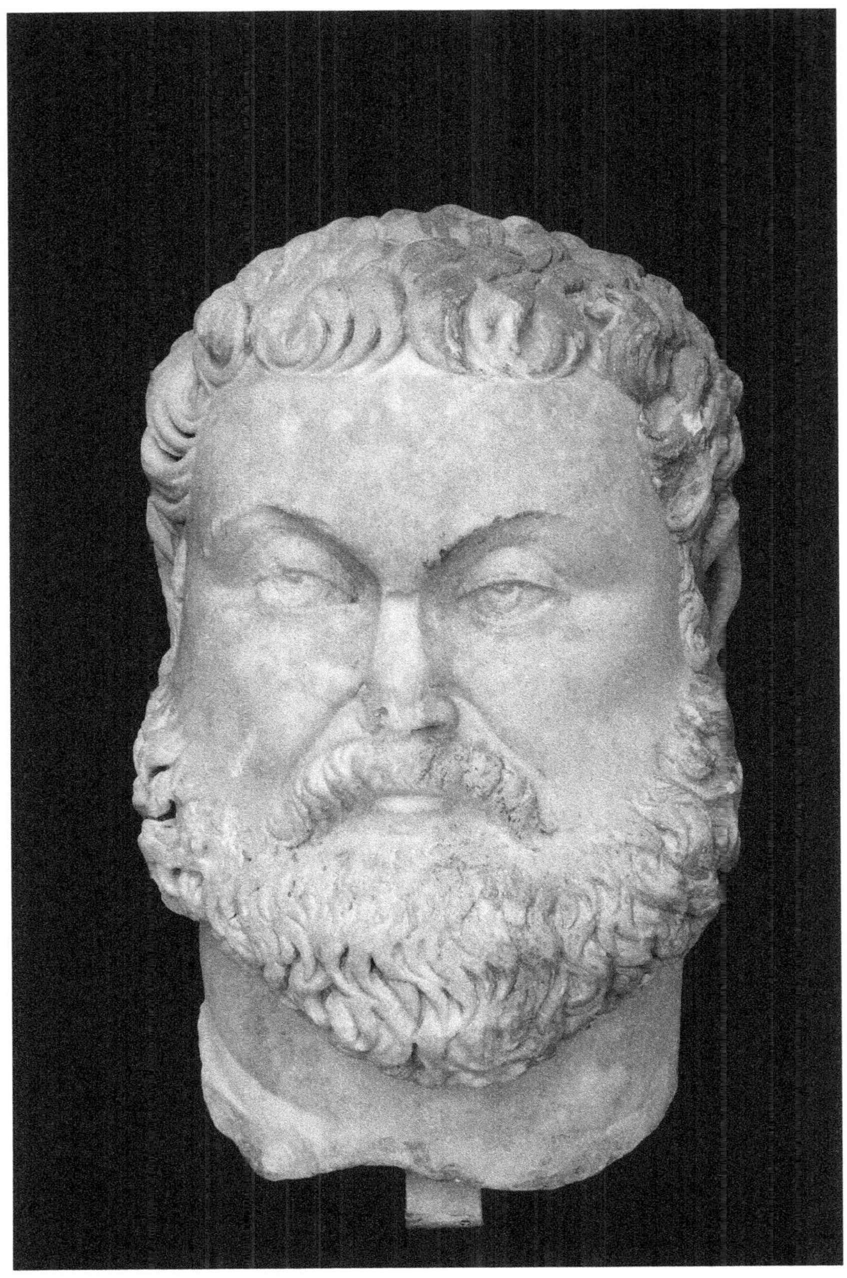

Figure 10

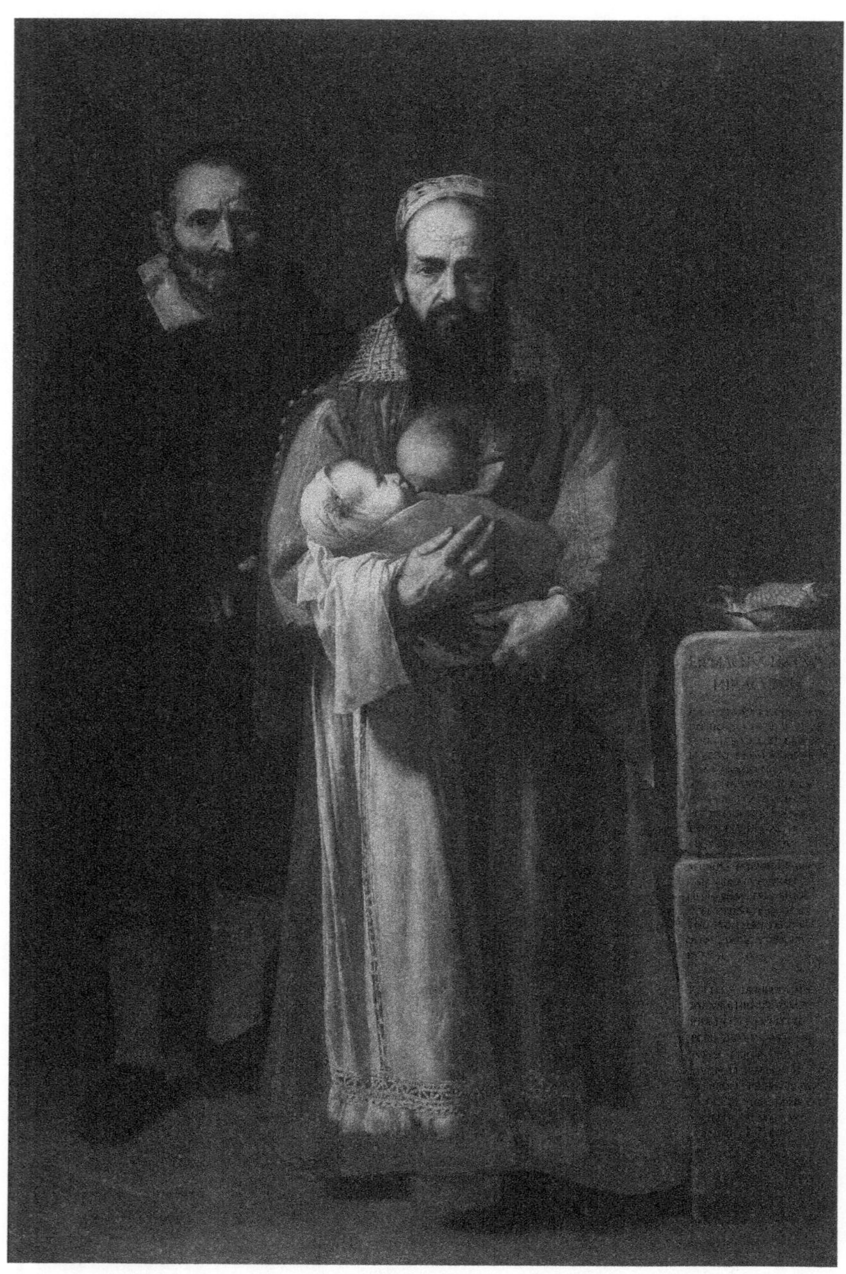

Figure 11

term that must be understood here both in the sense of the image, painting, or photo, and in the sense of the "character or appearance" of the person represented—and it gives this tone in such a way that the portrait "itself," if one dares say such a thing, becomes a real person or "the" real person. That is why we might say of an Avedon photograph, "this portrait of Marilyn is a little nervous" or indeed, "Marilyn looks a little nervous here."

Theophany

In its weaving of Judeo-Greek themes, Christianity introduced a revolution into the *mimesis* of the human face and from there into *mimesis* in general. If man is made in the image of God, on the one hand, and if, on the other hand, God becomes man—that is, if God makes himself into his own image but within the mortal condition defined through its sin—then the image of man can oscillate between divine value and the value of human fallenness.

In principle, the image of God is the image of the invisible of which it is forbidden to make an image. But we must not confuse the "first" image with the "second." There is a series of considerations to be made here, as much regarding the different theologies as regarding the semantics of Hebrew, Greek, and then Latin. Without dwelling on it, we could content ourselves with the following: Man is "image" in the sense of "resemblance" while the painted or sculpted "image" that supposedly (re)presents (a) god is an "idol" (a Greek term belonging to the family of words denoting vision but used to translate a Hebrew term that is, in fact, different from the one signifying resemblance). Man's resemblance to an invisible god consists of a resemblance to his activity—man pursues creation by peopling the earth—and does not involve a reproduction of the divine presence. By contrast, the idol is the object (not necessarily figurative) to which one attributes a divine quality and to which, as a consequence, one could address prayer and respect. It is in the former, non-idolatrous sense that the true god is not (re)presentable.

The son of God, on the other hand, the man Jesus, is representable—at least that is how the violent crises of iconoclasm would finally be resolved. Of course, he is not representable in terms of the features of the historical person, which are unknown. However, he is representable either in terms of the features of a man who is chosen to be a model, or in terms of a face composed in accordance with a certain idea or ideal of what this divine humanity must have been.

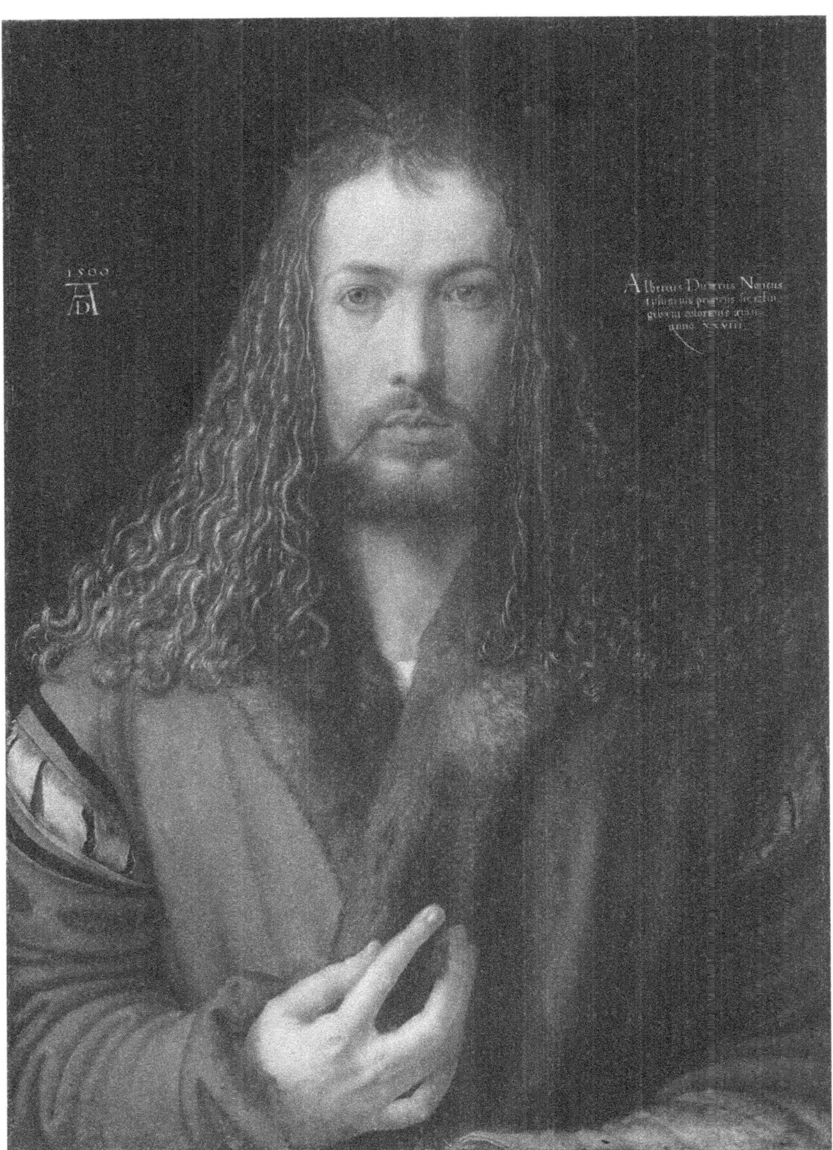

Figure 12

In the year 1500, Albrecht Dürer did a self-portrait in which he gave himself certain attributes designated by the tradition as Christ-like (the hair, the clothing, the hand gesture) (Figure 12). His aim, which could easily have been taken as impious or even blasphemous, could on the contrary have arisen—in the age of the first humanism, shortly before the Reformation—from a

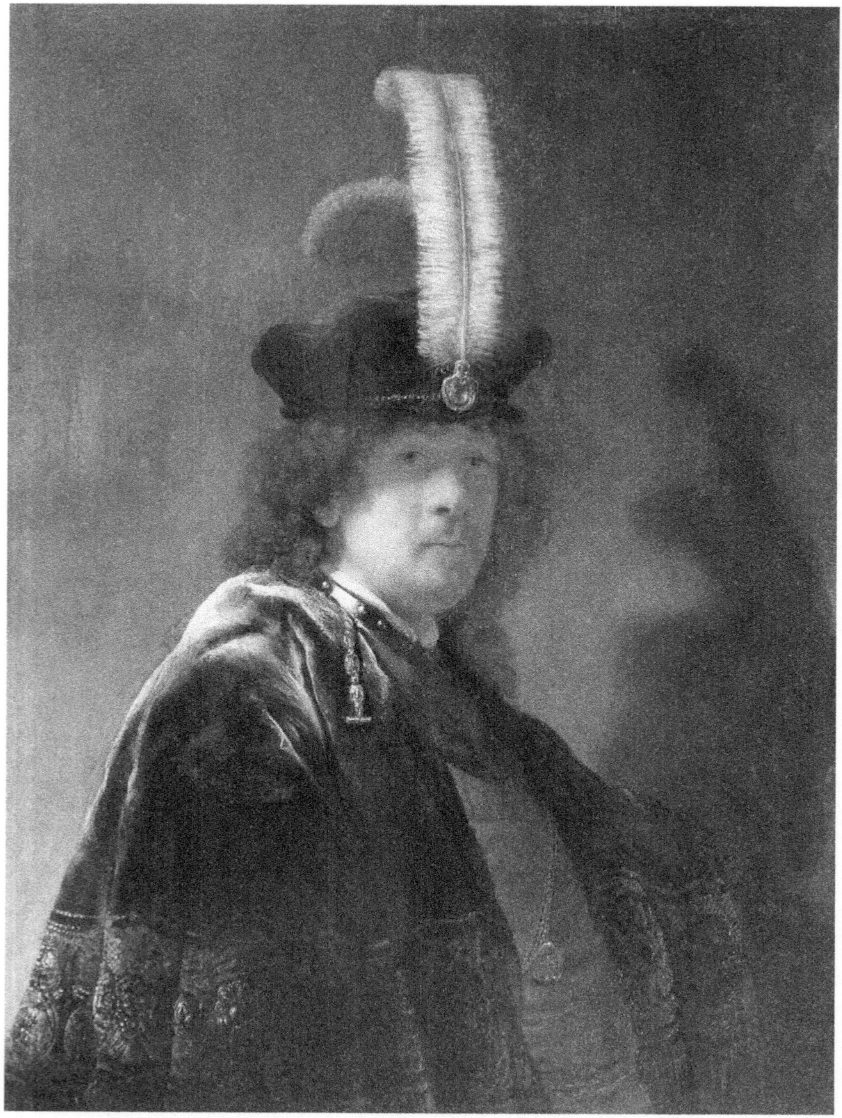

Figure 13

spiritual theology according to which every man participates in the mystery of the incarnation and the incarnation attains its full truth even there, in the portrait of a man.[1] This theology brings about an aesthetic: If, on the one hand, it is clear that there is no portrait of Christ, on the other hand, it is no less clear that the portrait of a man opens onto something of the divine, and most singularly in the portrait of the painter if, by painting, this very painter rekindles the gesture of creation or even receives his art from God himself (for such is indeed the thought that Dürer articulates in certain writings). This theophanic self-portrait seems to be the threshold of the history of art in full possession of its concept but it also articulates a crucial issue: Either the subject can see itself or be seen in God (according to the two possible meanings of the expression, *se voir*), or else it risks not being seen at all.

With the Reformation, a double movement is then produced that bears witness to the tremor that occurs within *mimesis*: On the one hand, it is well-known that German and Flemish painting affirms the presence of man in the world and on the other hand, an iconoclastic gesture is replayed that sometimes extends to the point of destroying or, what is indeed a remarkable detail, enucleating the looks from images of God, Christ, or the saints. The quest for the *autos* tends to be found somewhere between the extremes of a figuration without transcendence and an un-figurable transcendence, or else also between a man who is indistinguishable from all those of his kind— indifferent resemblance—and the exceptional man whom the spirit penetrates—resemblance of difference itself. In the meantime, politico-religious or socio-theological battles are spreading and becoming more intense, due to the printing press and the proliferation of portraits intended either to celebrate or to debase (through caricature) the images of the principal characters.[2]

Perhaps we can experience some of this tension in Rembrandt's pursuit of a quasi-interminable variety of self-portraits in which he continually *makes himself* other (in the two senses of "making a rendering of himself" and "transforming himself"): Other than a self in itself, he becomes rabbi, philosopher, Turk, old woman ... (Figure 13).

Revelation

Much later, an artist like Urs Lüthi sets about representing the many stages of his own transformation from a young man into an old woman (Figure 14).[1]

What has changed most from Rembrandt to Lüthi could well be the affective tone of the portrait. In the case of Rembrandt, this tone remains in the register of an affirmation whose self-confidence is not seriously shaken by suspicions of anxiety which, whatever their possible legitimacy, are going to be sought more behind the painting than in it, in rumors about personal psychology. In the case of Lüthi, on the other hand, by going through the phases of transformation, he specifically paints a disquiet or doubt on the subject of who is seeing him- or herself being seen and who no longer recognizes him- or herself as a consequence.

But for all that, Lüthi's doubt or trembling does not amount to the representation of a psychology. It is not a matter of psychology: It is a matter of a displacement of the schema of *mimesis* and, within that mimesis, of the form that was upholding and beckoning the portrait. This displacement is doubtless already there in the work of Rembrandt; in fact, perhaps it has always already worked the formal element of mimesis, more or less secretly. The "crisis" of "representation" and the destabilization or abandonment of figuration are not simply events that have occurred in contemporary history, in the broad and historial sense of the term. As the sequence and the movement of our account make clear, they are forces that have been in play since the formation of the mimetic regime. The portrait, ever a "self-portrait," contains at its origin the difficulty, if not the contradiction, of the *autos* that cannot position itself without finding itself to be other and that would only exist through the gesture of placing itself in front of itself. The statue of Apollo is indeed god himself, as Pessoa claims, but this god in the image of man already unsettles man, who could therefore only be a mute statue, an idol . . .

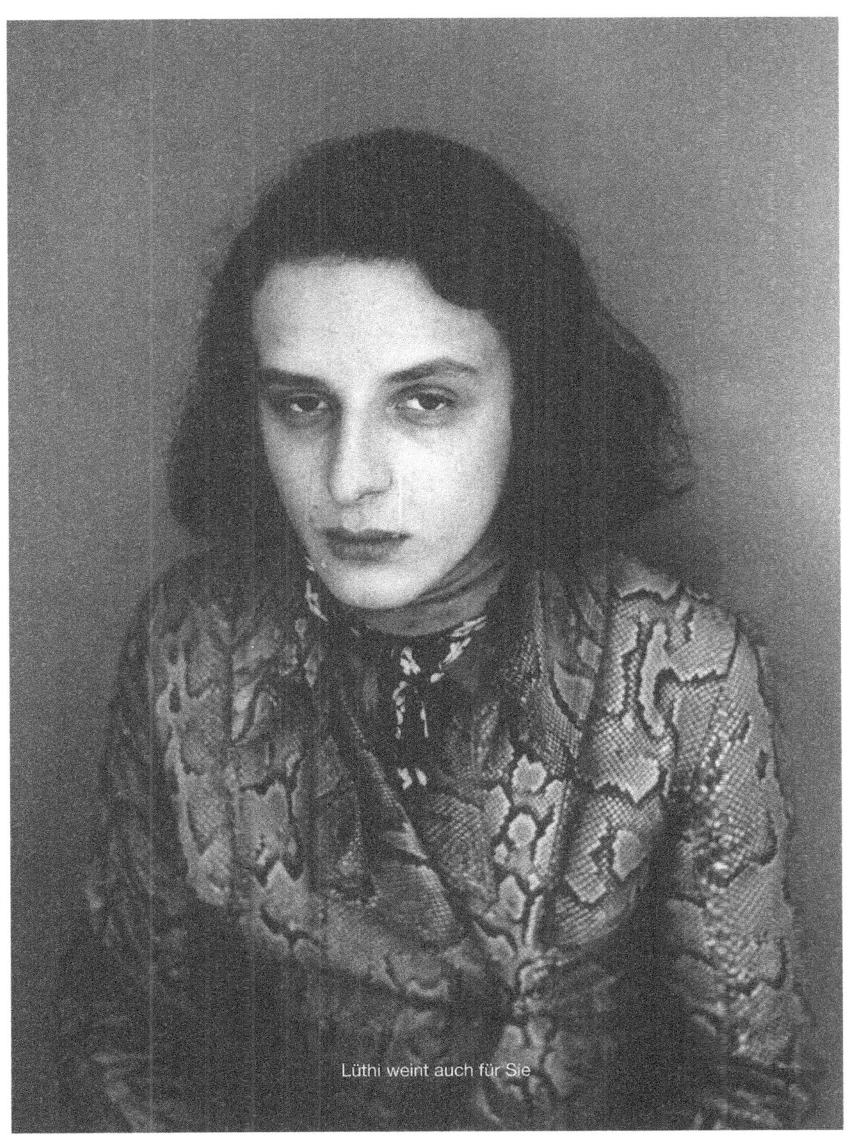

Figure 14

That is why the god-become-man named Jesus Christ corresponds to an intensified renewal of the mimetic expectation in that he provokes the singular quest for a portrait that would be neither mimetic nor artistic but would involve the very impression of the face itself: This is the legend of the veil of Veronica, whose name sets off the play on words *"vera icona."* The true image, or the genuine image[2]—which we could also call the automatic image—is that whereby the *autos* presents itself through itself, without mediation or figuration, and that involves the trace left by means of actual contact. But this trace creates the image, which means that although that it is not representative, it is still turned toward a spectator and is, in short, destined for him or her: The supposed immediacy of the image shows itself to be created via a detour destined to guarantee the representation by neutralizing its figural value and preserving the values of authority and of an appeal to the viewer.

The phantasm of the genuine image is only created to bring out more fully the impossibility of a visible attestation to "itself." The form that we could call *auto-poetic* (or auto-productive) and *auto-iconic* that silently governs the portrait at the heart of *mimesis* is disturbed and finally breaks down: The autonomy of the subject places itself in doubt—it is, at base, the extreme act by which it affirms itself by deposing itself—and with this doubt "the figure of man" begins to move aside.[3]

Let us make no mistake: The "death of God" is, above all else, the disappearance of man, of an ideal form of man as subject—of the world, of history, of self, of its image and thus of its presence no less than of its absence. The other—that of which portraits are made—conspicuously escapes sameness: Such is perhaps already the lesson of Rembrandt, but it is certainly that of Cézanne's *Self-Portrait with Palette* (Figure 15). The resemblance of the features and the posture to those of the painter seems above all to serve to mark out the space of an immense and intense eruption of light, perhaps an evocation of the golden backgrounds of the Italian Primitive school and Byzantine icons, or of the golden light that bathes the face of the subject of Dürer's *Self-Portrait* from 1500 (Figure 12).

But here the "self" of the painter withdraws into its (re)presentation in some way openly, for in this, the (self-)portrait only serves as a pretext—recalling a tradition—for a strong coloration that is not at all the background but is the true substance of the painting. For it is not a matter of reproducing this color, this yellow (exceptionally radiant in Cézanne), but of producing it, as color and space—color and space that are not uniform but given in variations, nuances, and contrasts that make up their proper topography. We could say that this "proper" is that which takes the place of the proper autonomy of a subject.

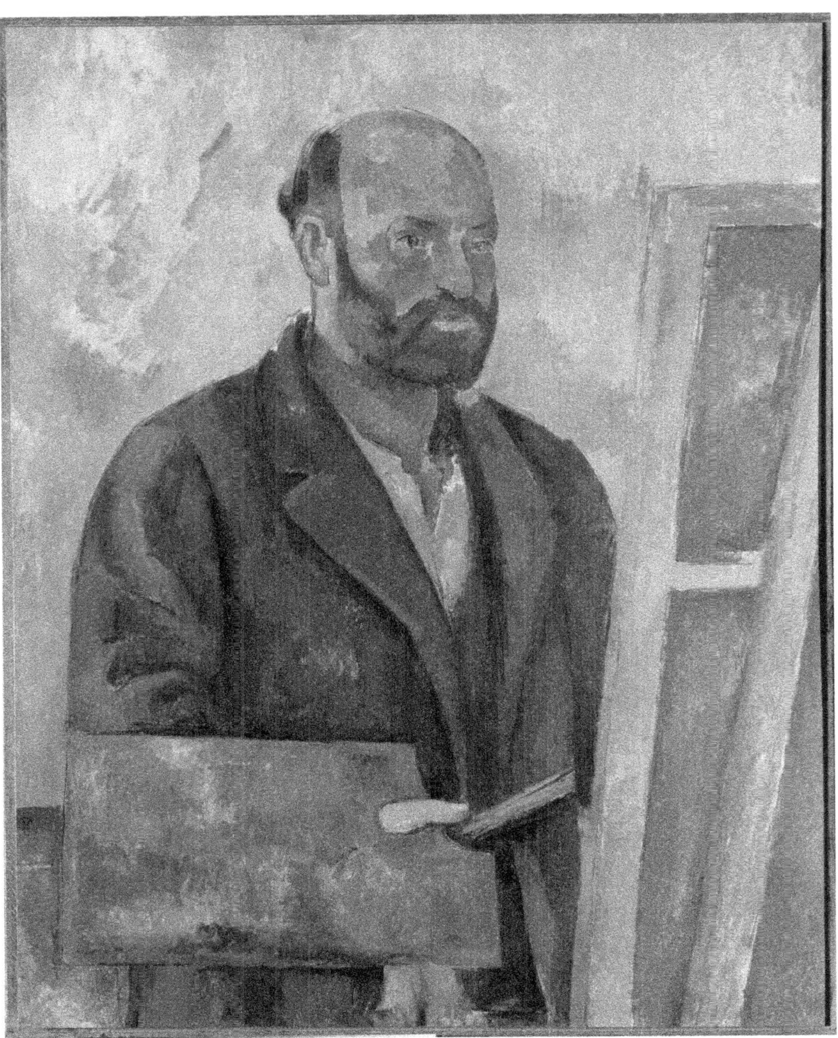

Figure 15

It is no doubt important to emphasize that the subject is always-already withdrawn and othered (indeed, alienated, become estranged, or else unnerved). Nevertheless, its withdrawal could—and should—open onto a mystery, according to the logic of the *interior intimo* opened up (and then shut down again?) by Augustine. According to a value that is as ancient as it is Christian, the mystery is the process of an unveiling (even if, in the mode of Christianity at the very least but perhaps also in every mode, it unveils a veiling that is renewed to infinity). "Revelation" not only involves the lifting of a veil, but much more involves the showing of the veil itself as light: What is veiled is shown as veiled and is shown in the truth of the veil that adheres to the "thing" underlying it, that is, to the "subject," the veil dissimulating it and situating it, designating its form in a vague outline, its presence in its imminence, its attraction in its withdrawal.[4]

Within a regime of revelation (regarding which once again, one can consider Christianity as a limit, not an absolute novelty), the mystery inherent to the withdrawal holds in reserve a superior clarity. As is the case with Dürer's face, the subject lights up with a divine light that is identical to that of the painting (gesture of the painter, artistic material, invention, emotion) and that of man (this man, as all men). This light is neither explanatory nor demonstrative—it is not cognitive—but it is monstrative and it is a thinking light: It thinks itself in showing itself (so, this light is *cosa mentale* according to the famous phrase for what Dürer had learned so well). *Mimesis* thinks itself here in its truth without a given model and whose true model is in its very execution.

Once more, Rembrandt's work is perhaps the moment of redirection where the revelation of the (self-)portrait *veers*, if it is possible to put it in such a way. It does not abolish itself; it does not lose itself either in the darkness or in the glare (or in a loss or triumph of "man"); but it does remain indecisive between a still-divine possibility and another for which the "human" is no longer self-evident (let us not forget Rembrandt's *Anatomy Lessons*).

That which was, as mystery, the spontaneous and *self*-sufficient clarity and apparent thinking of a subject or the exposure of an autonomy becomes a fleeting enigma, an irreducible complexity, a disquieting or grotesque strangeness (autonomy or anatomy?). Goya's portraits are the first witnesses to a realism wherein the iconic majesty of the princes becomes clouded and the sufferings of war, madness, and misery are conveyed. In this regard, the "realism" signifies less the precise rendering of an objective observation than the mimesis of an opacity, indeed, of an impenetrability of the real—a real that is not that of a face without being at the same time that of its sociality, its confrontations, and its exposure to others.

The subject *veers*, we could say once more—the subject, the individual, the *socius*, man finally. He veers from the clear to the obscure, from the distinct to the confused. As Baudelaire's poet recounts it, he has lost his halo:

> Well, just now as I was crossing the boulevard in a great hurry, splashing through the mud in the midst of a seething chaos, and with death galloping at me from every side, I gave a sudden start and my halo slipped off my head and fell into the mire of the macadam. I was far too frightened to pick it up.[5]

Divine Abandonment

The loss of the halo in Baudelaire could have as its equivalent in painting the numerous skulls painted by Cézanne, often alone ("autonomous") but sometimes accompanied by a portrait. The bony skull had previously been a preferred symbol for "vanity." Once divorced from the discourse of religion, the skull now seems to qualify the subject not from the perspective of its destiny but in terms of what is happening with its presence. So, one might suggest that, for the portrait, the halo—the possibility, very simply, of a divine dignity or a consecration—was nothing other than the possibility of painting the presence deep within the subject, be it a mysterious presence or indeed precisely in its mystery (a mystery that is as social, hierarchical, or heroic as it is personal, spiritual, or sensual).

So we need to understand how it is the same movement that both disrupts the portrait and turns painting upside down, as Cézanne does (not only him, and not all of a sudden, but we can content ourselves with using his name in this context). Painting, and with it photography, passes—if we can put it thus—from sensibility to sensation (this word that is so very Cézannian): That is, after painting has seized on and elaborated forms and values, comes a confrontation with the obscure thickness of a real, where it is a matter both of extracting and producing what is called "sensation," but which is only sensation in also being "conception" and "construction." One could again try to describe this in the following way: The composition is no longer that of the painting but that of the real (and this is equally true for photography, as it will be for film).[1]

Simultaneously therefore, the portrait no longer has to capture a mystery offered deep within a face, and painting/photography[2] no longer has to seize and interpret the delicate play of light and shadow, hues, and models. For that matter, this simultaneity must surely be based on identity: that of a *mimesis* in some way assured of the identity and properness of a model,

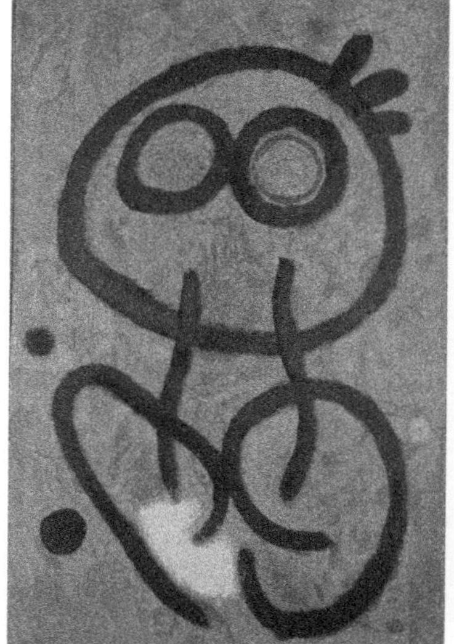

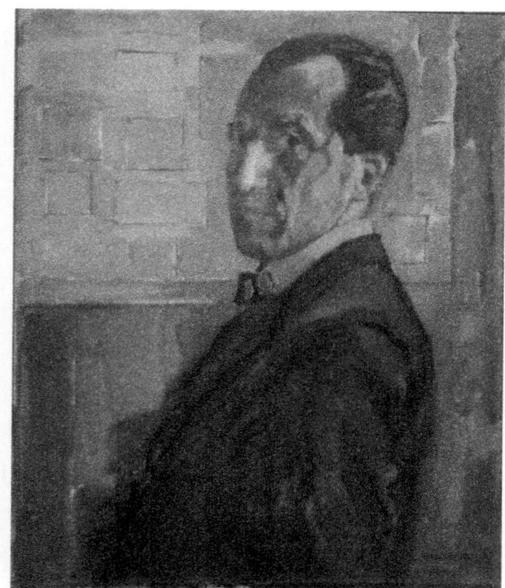

Figure 16   Figure 17

however divinely infinite in their ultimate content they may be. In contrast, henceforth the *mimesis* that knows itself without recourse to a model does not reproduce but rather produces itself (in the strongest sense of the word): It carries itself outside, in front, ahead of itself, not in the sense of a view set before a gaze but in the sense of a vision that emerges from the gaze in order to be formed and find itself outside.

That is how *mimesis* begins to know itself expressly without recourse to a model, becoming on the contrary its own model, that is, itself *modeling itself* (which is not a play on words, since "model" and "to model" proceed from the same semantics of *modus*, the measure in accordance with which adjustments are made).

If representation models itself, if it represents itself (depicts itself, appeals to itself, authorizes itself), this means that representation itself becomes "subject": There is no longer a subject of the representation nor is there a representation of the subject. That is how a self-portrait could become the outline of a face treated in a style proper to painting, as for example Miró does in his 1937 self-portrait (Figure 16). Or else, that is also how a self-portrait could present the face as inseparable from a non-figurative style, as is the case with Mondrian's 1918 self-portrait (Figure 17).

A sort of "self-portrait" of painting/photography itself doubtless marks a fairly significant moment in the history of the portrait in the first half or first two-thirds of the twentieth century. However, Artemisia Gentileschi had already represented herself as the allegory of painting. It could be that the painting of a portrait and the portrait of painting have always been more or less secretly tied to one another. Still, it is no less the case that the history of the portrait as such proceeds by unraveling the thread of *mimesis*, and when painting represents itself to itself freed from figuration, it is then accompanied by a powerful questioning of the human figure—which also means, more precisely, a questioning of the possibility of considering this figure in terms of something like a divine mystery, though of course a thoroughly secular one.

Henceforth, a mystery or enigma will not appear by virtue of a resemblance to the human figure. What is playing itself out here is a question of the "human," a question of art, and a question of the "mystery" as such, that is, of the possibility of an expression of the impenetrable or the unpresentable—of a "soul," if not of a divine secret.

Dis-figuration

It is against this backdrop that we need to differentiate the strictly contemporary that is both our subject and where we are ending up—the turn of the twentieth century to the beginning of the twenty-first—from the "contemporary" that has already been, if one may say so, registered as such. In terms of the portrait, this distinction could be characterized in terms of the various kinds of surplus enigma—to recover the term that we have distinguished from the mystery. Rather than devoting the time required for a detailed study of these terms, we will have to content ourselves with invoking them in a somewhat elliptical fashion.

Of course, this history unfolds against the background of the deployment of what is called "abstraction" or, more appropriately for our purposes, "non-figuration," in which we can discern the continuation of a movement initiated by Cézanne as well as Malevich. By definition, non-figuration excludes the portrait, even more so than other kinds of figuration. It is particularly remarkable that in precisely this context, the portrait continues to be sought after.

Whether it be a question of "abstraction" or of all the other ways in which the standards of traditional figuration have been displaced, disrupted, or called into question, a demand or concern regarding the portrait regularly returns—and in a particularly insistent manner if one compares the portrait to the landscape or the still life, not to mention scenes of whatever kind. The question of *mimesis* continues to be posed to its subject or through it, and this remains the case even when the genre might seem to be dominated by the photographic portrait. For, the photographic portrait only dominates in precisely one of two ways: either by restricting itself to the portrait's documentary function or, on the contrary, by treating the portrait in accordance with a questioning of the enigma of the subject, which leads the photograph back toward painting.

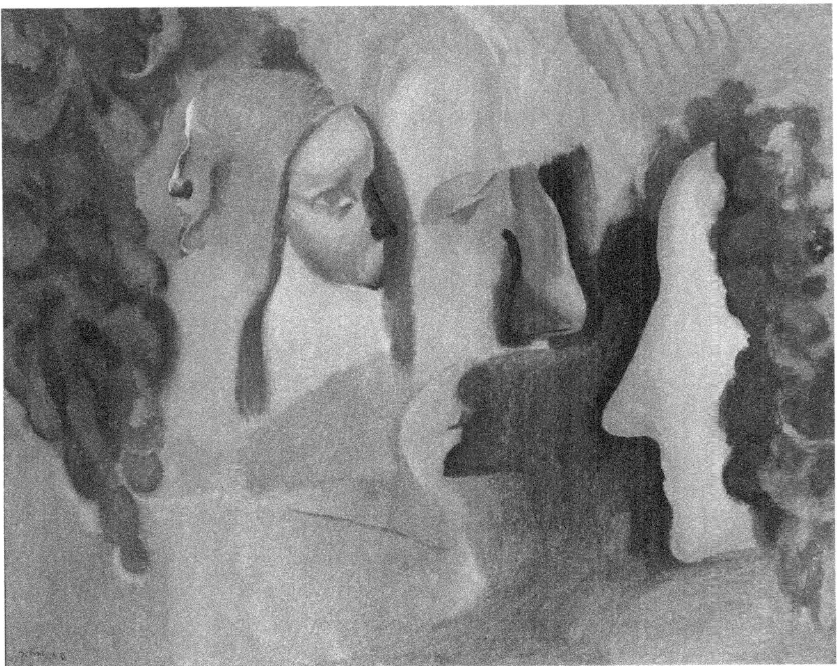

Figure 18

When the mimetic demand speaks to the very heart of *mimesis*, the human figure, under the regime of divine abandonment on the one hand and of non-figuration on the other, the portrait cannot avoid being exposed to disfiguration, or at times to over-figuration. Picasso will have provoked so much commentary on the inhumanity of his human figures that it would be useful to return to it. As for over-figuration, one may find it in several varieties of hyper-realism: in paintings done from photographs, or else in the overwhelming increase of saturated images used for advertising that attempt to evacuate all subjectivity or all presence.

In 1911, Duchamp painted a canvas with the forceful title *Yvonne and Madeleine Torn to Tatters* (Figure 18). This "tearing to tatters," the decompositions, deconstructions, and disfigurements of the human figure—and therefore also of the portrait—will continue throughout the history of the twentieth century. This is well-known and need not be rehearsed here. What matters here is the convergence—through conjunctions, parallelisms, and intersections—of transformations and upheavals that span European civilization as such, and that are nearly impossible to divide up into supposedly distinct areas like "aesthetics," "politics," or "philosophy." It is a question of the subject's relation to itself under all the various guises it might assume (social, symbolic, psychic, sensory, and so on), so it is also a matter of the "figure" in all of its meanings. The visibility of a face, the epiphany of a "consciousness" or "spirit," the shaping and fabrication of models: All of this is taken into a maelstrom at the heart or hollow of which the very idea of what we might call, following Freud, the "ego ideal" or the "ideal ego" disappears.[1]

Furthermore, by introducing these ideas, Freud represents the intersection of all the lines of force that traverse the human subject, which he declares to have suffered three great wounds in the modern age. These bear the names of Copernicus (the end of geocentricism), Darwin (the animal origin of mankind), and Freud himself (the limits and the weakness of consciousness). But it is not enough to remain at the level of what in the same text he calls "the narcissistic illusion." In the collapse of the possibility of a face-to-face of the "self," another issue arises—it goes without saying—that involves the profound renewal of what had always created a mystery, an enigma, or a secret of the *same* as recognition of the self. We have claimed that the *other* had earlier functioned as the imagined "divine" in the *mimesis* of the human body-face. Now it makes itself known (if we may use this word) simultaneously as no longer bearing the hallmarks of an essential or indeed supreme being (such as God could have been conceived in a monotheistic regime, that is, however much it tends toward the an-iconic), *and* as the bearer of a mystery that is ultimately more mysterious, more unfathomable, and consequently more demanding, even more inflexible (more inhuman . . .) for the desire that seeks a face to look at.

Painting and photography therefore take part in an exploration of which neither psychoanalysis nor even philosophy strictly speaking is capable. What plays itself out with the *other portrait*, in the exercise we have begun here, is in effect a *withdrawal of the other* and therefore a *withdrawal of the portrait* (within the portrait "itself"). Fautrier's *Hostage Head*, painted in 1945, can be taken as emblematic here (Figure 19).

Along with the important and well-known analyses of this series of works by Fautrier—and other works by other painters or photographers of the same period (for example, *Broken Bench, Long Island* by André Kertesz) one must, of course, take note of the truly remarkable insistence on a human figure. This human figure not only persists and insists right up to its erasure, its distancing, and its blurring, but it still requires—that is to say, *anew, newly*—a look for which and through which the human figure should neither be stiffened into an ideal nor immersed into a dense "real," but should be *recognized* for what it bears—or what bears it—other than the completed identity of a form closed in upon itself.

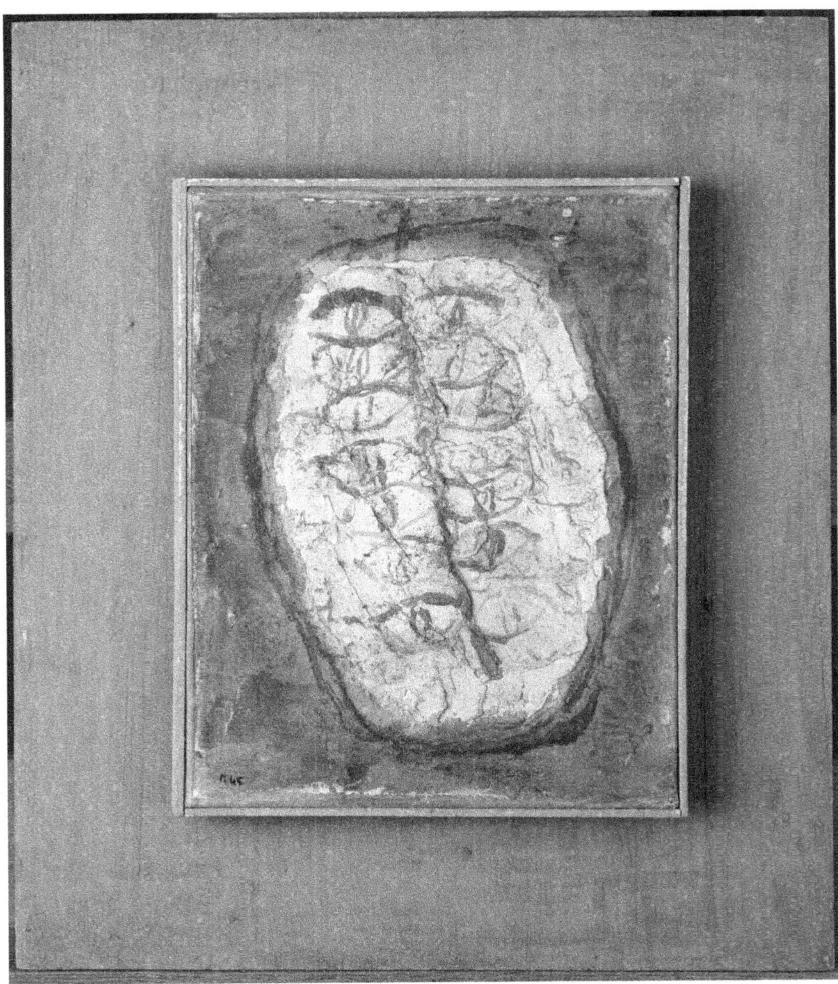

Figure 19

In a 1929 essay entitled "Human Face,"[2] Bataille could write that it is appropriate to "reduce the appearance of the self to that of the fly on the orator's nose." There is no better way to sum up a situation that can only be described, not as a "crisis," but as a complete trans-formation of the specifics of a culture and the bearings of a world. But if the trans-formation or "meta-morphosis of forms"[3] opens up the possibility of the shapeless [in-forme], it engages desire with no less force—not the desire to re-shape but the desire to probe the shapeless in the name of a "figure" that "would be incapable

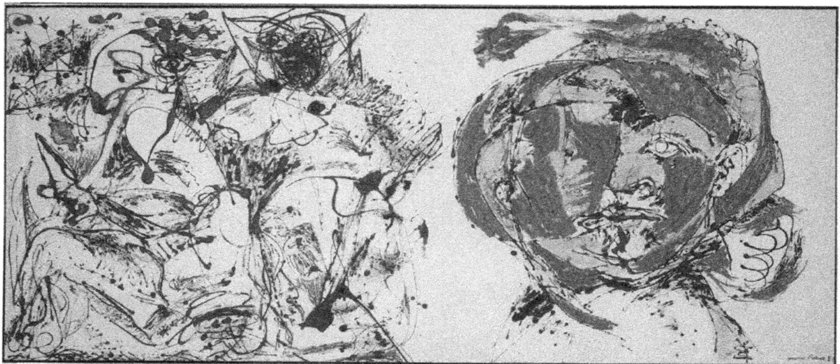

Figure 20

of making itself completely absent from our world."[4] In disfiguration, a transfiguration is sought, one that most certainly has nothing to do with the religious connotations of the word but that denotes the burst of a presence taken aback in absence, of a passing, of a dream where not the "fulfillment of a wish" but the real of a desire in action can be recognized. For example, the desire in action of Jackson Pollock's painting *Portrait and a Dream* (Figure 20).

We have to imagine that when divine figures are entirely effaced, when the arts can no longer base representation on mythological glory—whether that glory be religious, heroic, historical, or moral—the human figure, which had previously welcomed a glorious strangeness, stubbornly demands another recognition of alterity that it feels itself to bear and without which—be it deprived of glory, indecipherable, impenetrable—it could not attain the minimum of ipseity or selfhood needed to exist. As Alain Buisine wrote in 1992 about the persistence of the portrait (particularly in the work of De Kooning): "There is neither an abandonment of the figure nor a return of the figure, but simply the persistence of the inaugural vision"—a vision that De Kooning "himself called *a glimpse*, a fleeting, blurred, sidelong vision." And, as Buisine concludes: "Perhaps a face is precisely a face when we discover it in its truth: an impression that is as ephemeral as it is tenacious."[5]

Eclipse

The time and the movement of disfiguration—using this word as a kind of shorthand—continued, and continue to occur in various ways in our own time,[1] but we might suggest that they all have something in common in terms of a trans-figuration in the sense that I have just outlined: a passing, a transience and an uncertainty, the fragility of a light touch, or an allusion. The portrait does not seek to capture the identity of a figure, nor does it seek to capture identity within a figure: Rather, it allows for something to approach and recede, so that it is less a question of identity than of presence, in the sense that this latter cannot be identified with pure position, to a being-here that is duly located or assigned to its place but, in an entirely different way, *presents itself*, advances and appears in a happening that cannot be situated or fixed. The portrait remains immobile, certainly—and even the movement of a video camera does not take away from its withdrawal in which it by definition *takes place*—and nonetheless this stasis shows itself to be essentially dynamic, and even elusive, fluid, or volatile.

If the "other"—that is, him or her whose image we seek—withdraws in the portrait, in *its* portrait, it is not so much to harbor the secret of a mysterious or fascinating identity in the depths of this withdrawal, as it is to share with those of us who look at it the strangeness that is only its own in being ours as well (Figure 21).

Two dimensions in particular may be inferred from this. On the one hand, the portrait accepts itself more explicitly as a portrait, and on the other hand, we seek in the portrait less a sameness or identity than we do an alterity or alteration of the identical.

That the portrait accepts itself more explicitly as a portrait is owing to the fact that it has rid itself of the extrinsic demands of figuration (the expression of a role, a power, and so on) as well as those of resemblance: We understand in an explicit way what the visual arts have always implicitly known—that is,

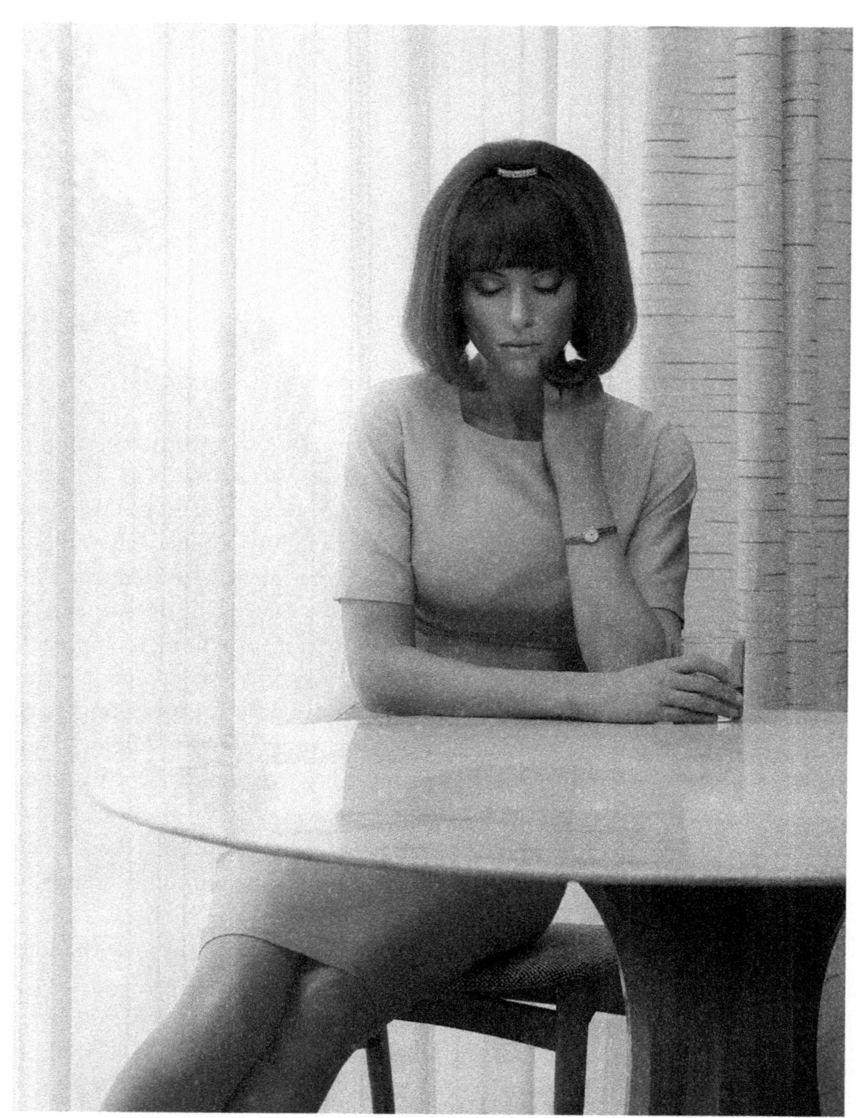

Figure 21

that *mimesis*, even when it refers to a model, does not seek out an imitation of morphological traits (of the *morphè*, which is the form given in outline), but rather that of the "interior" form, the "soul" of the model, a form called *idea*.[2] The "idea" is neither a notion nor a concept; it is the visible form (*idea* belongs to the Greek lexicon of vision) of that which is not initially given as appearance. The visible form, then, of that which much more offers itself as a *showing*—not appearing or seeming but coming-to-presence or self-showing. The image in its true value is not an illusion but nor is it a simple presence: It is an arrival, a movement, an advancing, or a rising from the depths.

This is more noticeable and more tangible for us today, but that does not mean that art has ever been able to ignore it: All the features of the arts of today have also shaped the arts of earlier times but according to other variations and other modulations. What is at stake today is a displacement of the subject in which the portrait is "rooted": The question of the contemporary portrait is the question of a subject who can no longer be the subject of a self-certainty or of a "humanism" gathering the properties of the divine into man.

It is also not a question of launching an attack against "man" but rather of asking oneself "how are the human face and the persistence of resemblance (which puts it together) [. . .] maintained in what would blow any other 'thing' to pieces?"[3]

For it is a question of a "thing": The portrait offers and in a sense places before us something that is not an object, but neither is it the pure eclipse by virtue of which a "subject" endlessly disappears in its very appearing (such an eclipse can take place as an utterance, a gesture, a glance). The portrait puts forth an appearing of disappearance: it retains this appearing while also submitting to it. That is why it ultimately has very little to do with "narcissism" in the common psychological sense of the word. Here, Narcissus must be understood as he who sees an image appearing in the water—in the uncertain and moving depths—that reproduces his gestures, that pleases and attracts him, but is not him. He appears without recognizing himself and if he recognizes himself, he no longer appears: He has withdrawn into his portrait.

The portrait forms the assemblage of appearing and disappearance, the silence between the two of an image that remains at the site of the eclipse, that presents its happening, its passing. Jean-Michel Alberola was able to declare: "It is Courbet who invented the modern self-portrait, where he is alone with his madness, while Poussin had represented himself in the midst of history, in the midst of other paintings."[4]

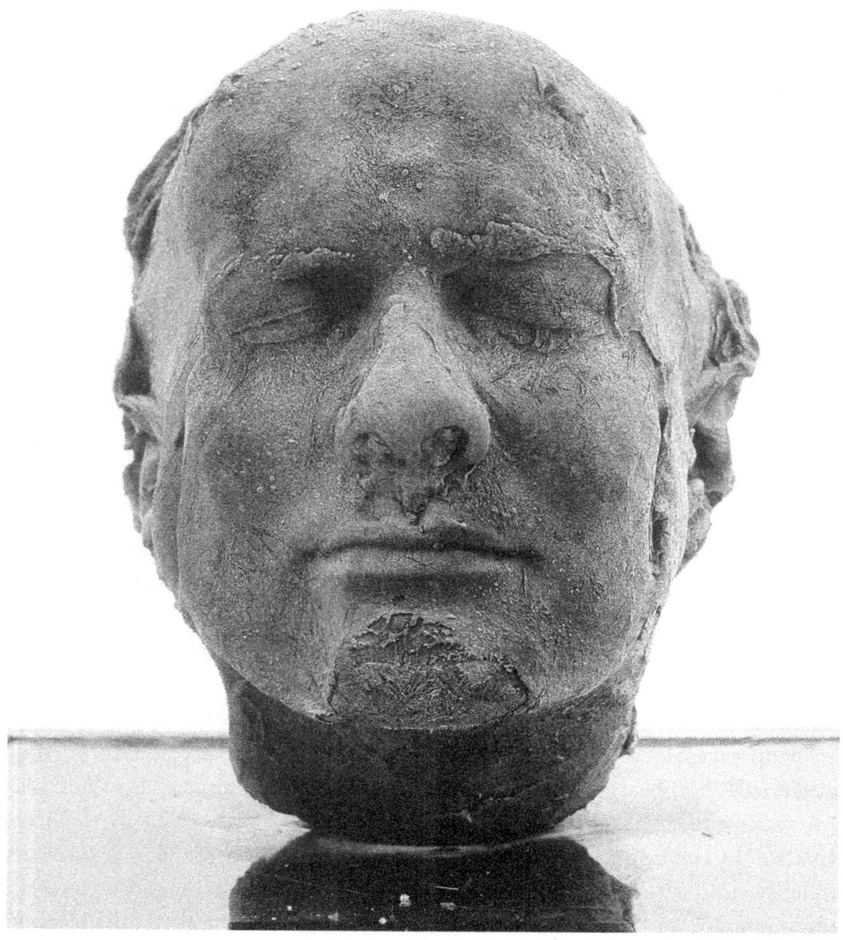

Figure 22

It is true that solitude and the eclipse of the subject can coincide with the height of "narcissism" or of literal identification, as it did for instance when Marc Quinn executed his self-portrait with his own frozen blood (Figure 22). But the literalness of "his own" here must be understood in an ironic way as well: The "real" blood in this case does not ensure the "authenticity" of the image any more than was ever the case with any holy shroud.

Infinite Detachment

The portrait no longer possesses an "authenticity" that is not placed on hold, at a distance, or in doubt. To put it in Heidegger's terms: "*Authentic existence is nothing which hovers over entangled everydayness, but is existentially only a modified grasp of everydayness.*"[1] The excellence of *mimesis* is no longer to be found in the likeness of the "self" to "itself," nor in the likeness of this "self" to the "me" who looks at it: It is much more to be found in a form of appealing to the viewer who is invited to act as the subject of their own look. As Max Imdahl writes: "The spectator contemplating the image is brought to an act of being-oneself by the mere fact of looking for his 'I' only in himself."[2] Imdahl's formulation does not seek to characterize the only possible relation to the portrait in contemporary art, but it is no coincidence that it finds its strongest resonance in the portrait.

Rineke Dijkstra shows us *Ruth Drawing Picasso* (Figure 23). This portrait of a schoolgirl focusing her every effort on representing a representation compels us to reproduce involuntarily the nervous pout of her careful attention, while at the same time we feel her tension and diligence, altogether worried, awkward, naive, and yet committed to this moment of instruction.

At the same time, Ruth is identified only by her first name, thus verging on an anonymity that is further emphasized by the plain school uniform. Anonymity and banality have in some way come to constitute an essential dimension of the portrait as soon as it has less to do with a morphological likeness than with a true semblance[3] or a veri-similitude [*une vrai-semblance*] that would be the expression or appearance of the essential form—the "idea"—albeit "essential," not in the sense of an ontological property, but on the contrary according to the existential meaning of the passing of a subject that never settles but that passes, and in passing, gestures to us. A common subject,[4] then, not identifiable in the sense of a "person" but in

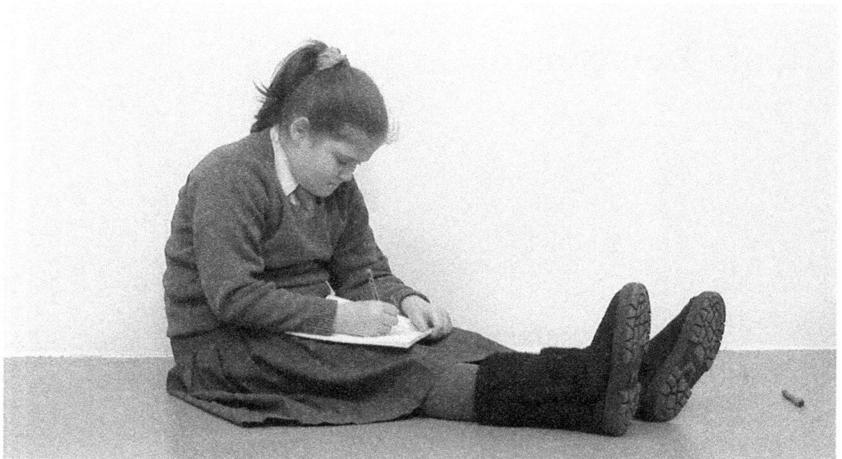

Figure 23

the sense of a singular identity taken in plurality, diversity, and common belonging, the interdependence of one another through which a familiar strangeness circulates, is divided and diffracted, a familiar strangeness of what seems to hesitate between subject and object, between presence and absence.

The *other portrait* is other than the portrait that proceeds from a presupposed identity, one whose appearance must be rendered. On the contrary, it proceeds from an identity that is hardly supposed at all, but rather is evoked in its withdrawal (Figure 24). This withdrawal takes on alterity in what one might call its absolute distinction, its infinite detachment with respect to any identification in both meanings of the word: the identity of self to self and identity of one self to another. Identification can neither be fixed nor presupposed, nor even deduced or concluded: It remains distant, floating, at once shared out and elusive.

Whereas *mimesis* was concerned with capturing the expression of a divine mystery of the human figure, trans-figuration concerns itself with an infinitely withdrawn face, absented within its own presence—"albeit without considering this presence (no presence at all, and therefore not the presence that the work of art is either) to be a given or something completely adhering to itself."[5]

Under these conditions, the portrait is the representation of the same that the other is in itself, only on the condition of being the presentation of the

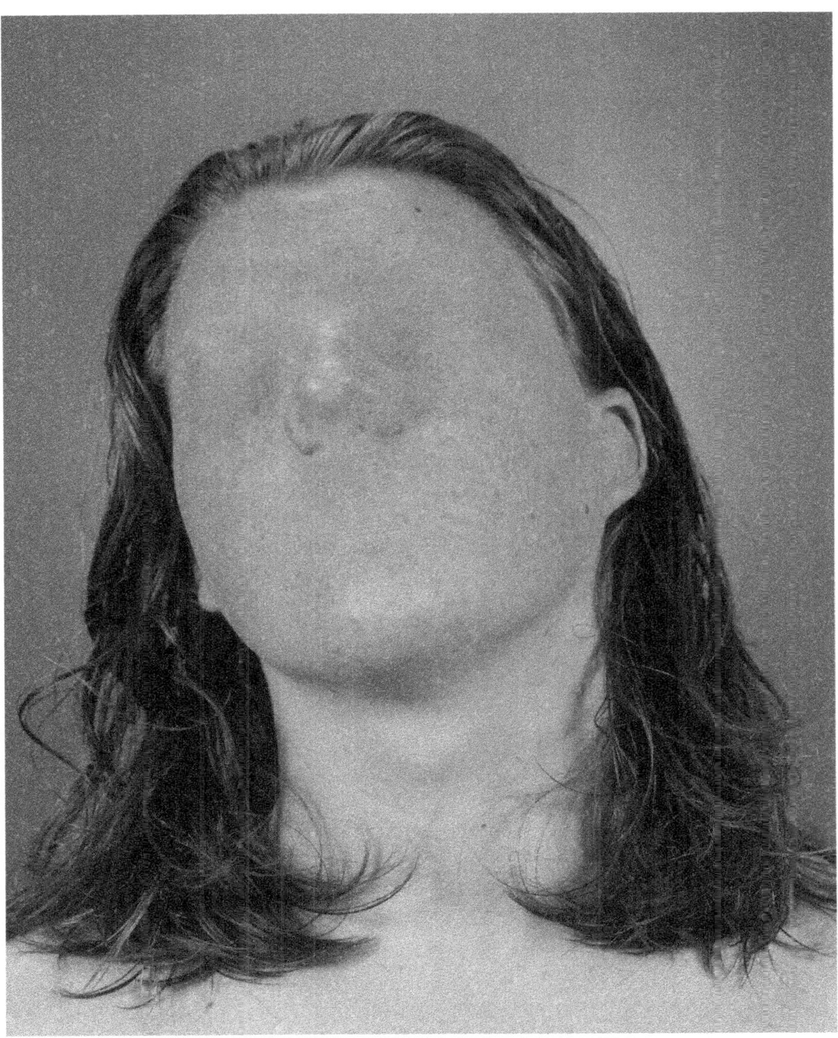

Figure 24

other that this other is, not only for me but equally as such and for itself. Sameness assumes alterity. Showing itself as other, the other withdraws to the depths of its portrait: The other absents itself in its self-relation, which, in a single movement, makes itself other for it as well as for us.

David Hockney's *Portrait of Nick Wilder* has its subject withdraw from the portrait by plunging him into a swimming pool and leaving him iso-

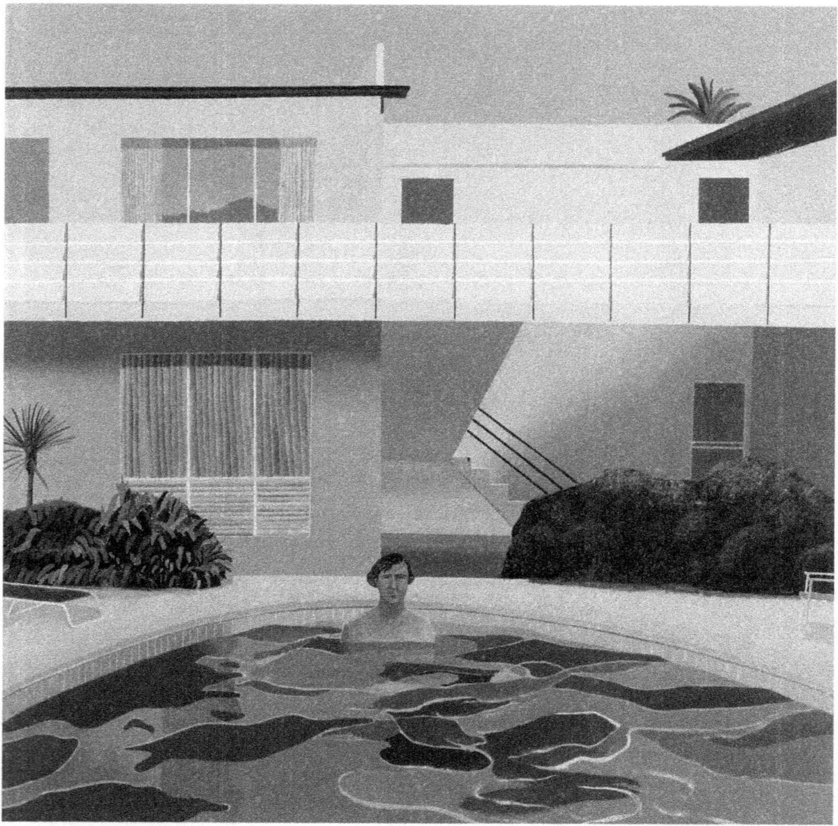

Figure 25

lated, as if lost in the midst of an environment at once luxurious and cold (Figure 25).

The torso, cut off by the surface of the water whose reflections receive the painter's utmost attention, corresponds closely to the classical cutting of a portrait, while the oval of the swimming pool and the many rectangles and squares of the building all serve to recall classic frames. Light is present mostly in the background and the face remains weakly lit, while a reflection in the water, which could be the drowning of the portrait, emerges and then is lost. But the figure adopts the necessary pose and looks very directly at the look—that of the painter, our own—that places him in the center of a painting from which he could, without serious consequences for the composition, be absent.

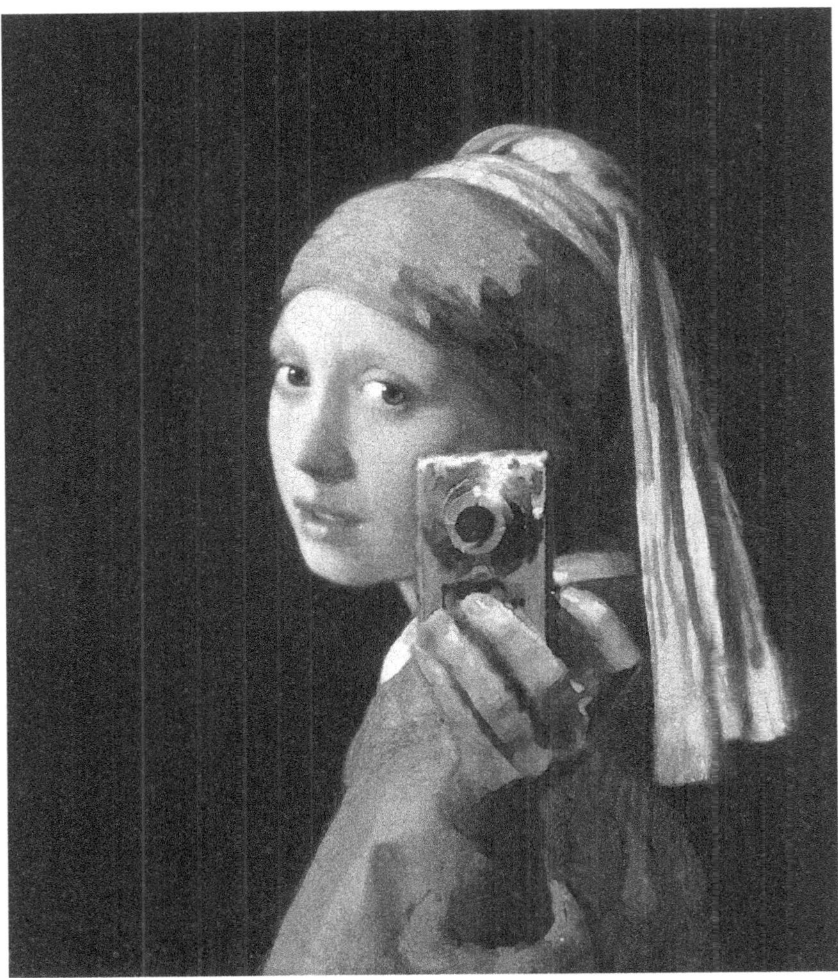

Figure 26

To sum up, we could say the following: Whereas the portrait used to have the task of representing the un-representable of the face, it must now bear witness to the passing, the fading away, and the uncertainty of a figure. At the same time, the portrait attests to the obsession, the awaiting, the desire (Figure 26), or else the swaying, the fluidity, and the drowning in the depths of the self (Figure 27).[6]

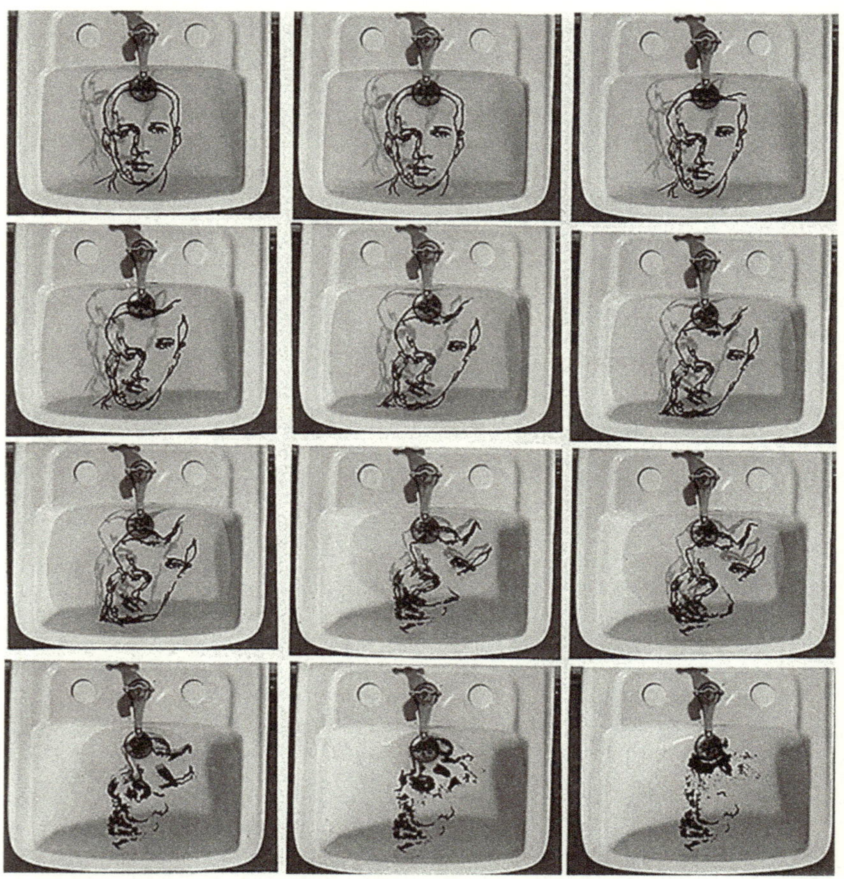

Figure 27

Coda I

Whether we designate the stakes of the portrait as the un-representable of the face, as the dis- or trans-figuration of the figure, or else as the indeterminate slippage of a face barely glimpsed, these diverse modes remain linked to each other by that which makes the portrait into the "absolute of the image."[1] The "absolute" designates that which is detached, *ab-solutum*, from everything. The image detached from everything is the image that bears no connection to a morphological referent (a model) but that offers the *idea*—to repeat it once more, the true "form," the coming to presence of a line or a flash, whose cut or clarity originates from afar, "high above ordinary existence," as Yves Bonnefoy puts it, alluding to the style of the Giacometti's portraits: "His great feverish intention to make the model exist, to 'sustain' it in being—and yet all the same, to sustain it above ordinary existence—gave birth to the trance."[2]

Bonnefoy discovers the motif of the trance in Giacometti's calmly and imperturbably agitated drawing, in the multiplication of traces, streaks, strokes, and lines, in the torrent of which a face emerges and withdraws, in short, from the *same drawn line* [le trait], from the line of its portrait/retreat [*por/ re-trait*]. As Merleau-Ponty writes in an entirely different context, "after all, a face is only shadows, lights, and colors."[3] This means that a face is a moveable play of reflections and angles, an essential instability that is always effacing or transforming itself.

This "essential" instability is equivalent to the absence of an essence, to the absence or incessant stripping away of a substance that is stable, permanent, and self-contained. This stripping away of the essence is called *existence*. What the portrait deciphers—in general, but more radically in its contemporary versions—is the truth of existence or existence as truth. *Ex-istence,* that is, the being-outside, the being out-of-itself, the passing-by that literally "represents" nothing, "imitates" nothing if not the very fact of passing-by itself,

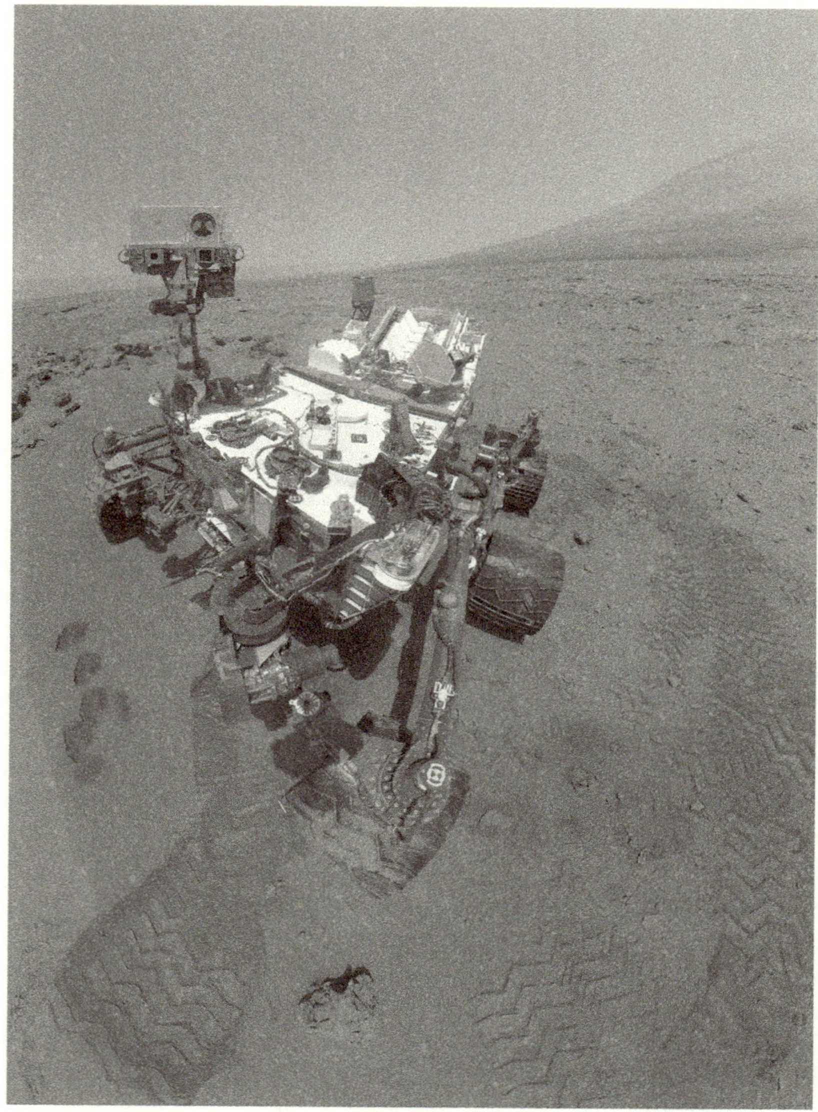

Figure 28

of coming and going, of ceaseless approaching and distancing, of allowing oneself to be recognized and of being mistaken for the inimitable (Figure 28), the indiscernable, or the indecipherable that existence is *and* that endlessly deciphers itself (at the risk of tearing itself apart) in portraits that are always other.

Coda II

One could say that, at the same time and in the same movement, the portrait both recedes from itself and draws nearer to itself. It recedes to the point of abandoning any morphological representation in favor of a *mimesis* that can specifically become that of an indeterminate gesture of representation where miracles, fantasies, death masks, or ancient divinities can return (Figure 29).

The portrait can also declare itself to be "vacant"—empty, open, free for whatever ectenic force (Figure 30). Or else, penetrating further into the theme of the "genuine image," it can try to go as far as an identity constituted on the basis of biochemical composition, as Marc Quinn does in his *Cloned DNA Self Portrait 26.c9.01* (Figure 31). Indeed, it can go as far as proposing to clone celebrities, where representation cultivates (in play, in irony, in sarcasm?) the ambition to transform itself into reproduction (thereby negating itself) (Figure 32).

In all of these and other ways, the portrait seems to want to exceed *mimesis:* to owe nothing more to any kind of model, to *model* itself on nothing or else to model itself on the nothing, as well as on the abstraction of an identity "in itself."

As the presentation of ideal figures and adequate images collapses, all these gestures amount to reaffirming, in an ever more insistent manner, the profound necessity that the portrait obeys (when it is not trapped in "authenticity" or its hollowed-out flipside): the exigency of allowing itself to be seized by the ever more distant, errant, and fascinating alterity and alteration of the one whom we cannot cease to imagine as a "self" and who withdraws their sameness into the depths of their image. But an image is indeed destined to do this, to show itself and to show the withdrawal of what it shows (Figure 33).

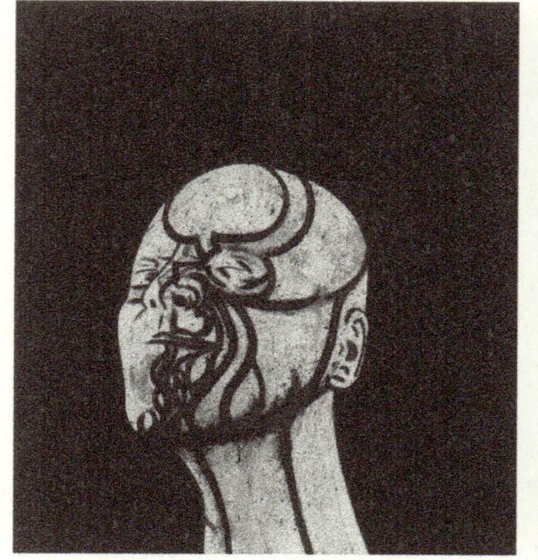

Figure 29

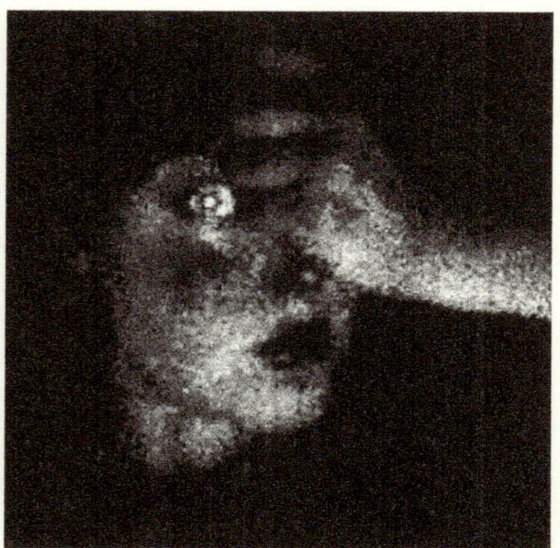

Figure 30

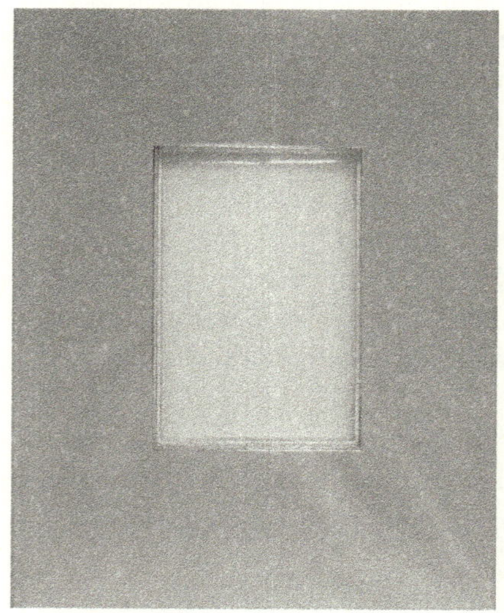

Figure 31

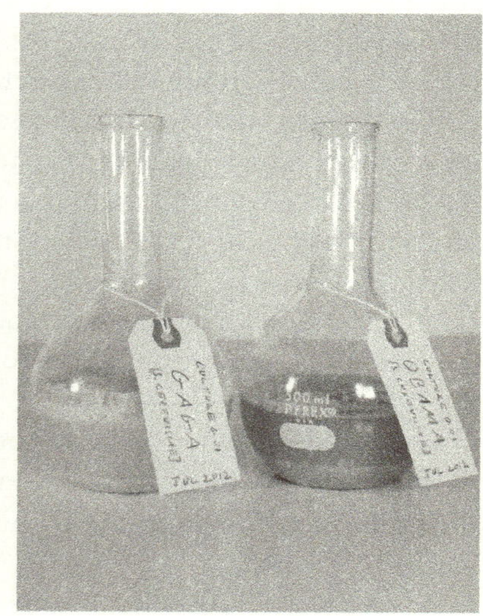

Figure 32

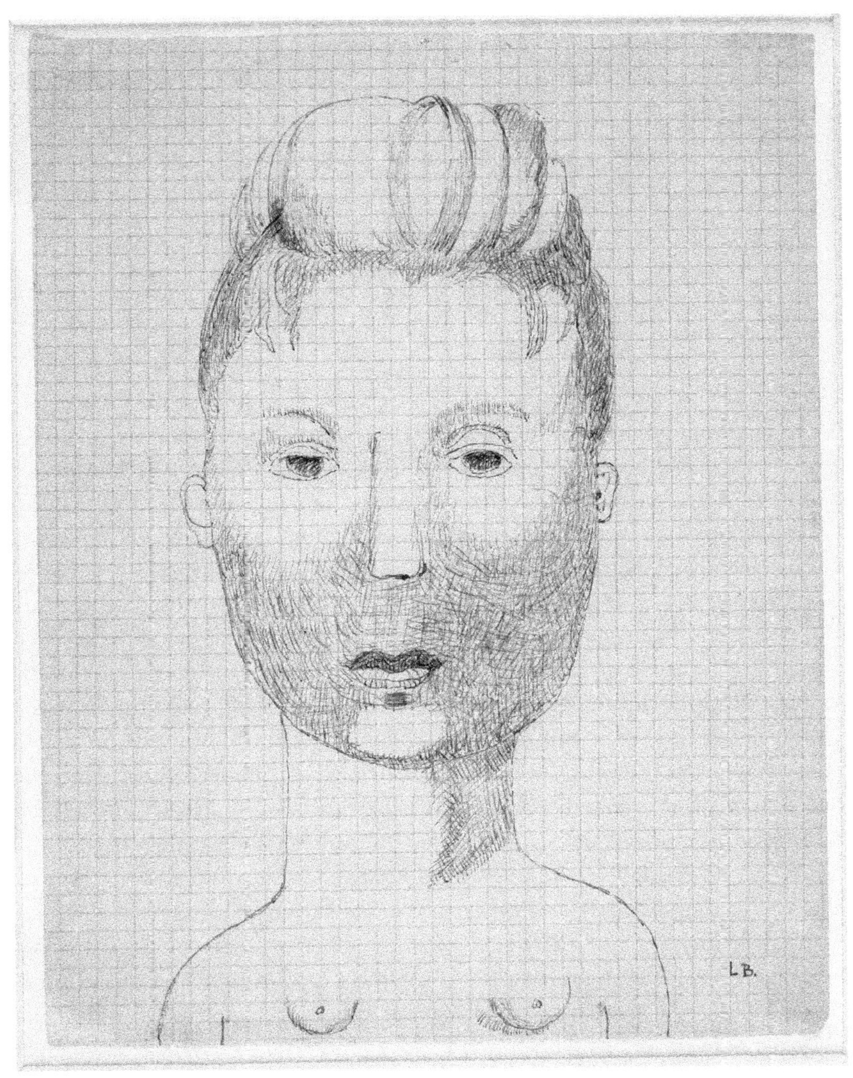

Figure 33

Coda III

The image and the portrait are thus intimately—or absolutely—linked. Every image is in search of, awaits, and demands an identity: the identity of a tree, a color, a face, whatever, for it is always a matter of that in which the "thing" is not only "what it is" but is *that which* it is. This *one, right here, properly its own*. It is not a matter of "properties" in the sense of attributes—not even essential attributes, as could have been said using the Aristotelian lexicon. But using the resources of that same lexicon, it is a matter of that which pertains to nothing other than itself, of the "substance" then, or the "individual," or more, of the being as such, not in its generality (which is how the word "being" is most commonly understood) but in the uniqueness that is inseparable from the being-self or being-such of any "being" [*étant*]. Nothing other than what modernity has named the "subject" (*a subject*) and whose history of the portrait shows us how it—the subject and/or the portrait; the subject in its portrait—never ceases to bring to light more and more of its character, which is both irreducible and *at the same time* inexpressible.

Concerning Rembrandt's self-portraits, Michel Guérin writes the following: "What Rembrandt paints is neither a position of 'me' (cherished, precisely because it belongs to him), nor the kind of status of which the subject could be proud: It is much more the *avoidance of the righteousness* of these traps and their curious transformation. Rembrandt does not ask: *Who am I then, me, the painted subject distinct from the subject that I claim to be?* He questions: *Quid* of the individual, at times paltry, at times pleasing, who comes to the image only for long enough to show how much it lets him down?"[1]

To which it suffices to add that this "letting down" [*le faux bond*] constitutes precisely the *true* leap [vrai *bondissement*] of both the subject and image, the gushing through which absence from self and in itself gives itself as presence to the world and to others (Figure 34). But this presence presents

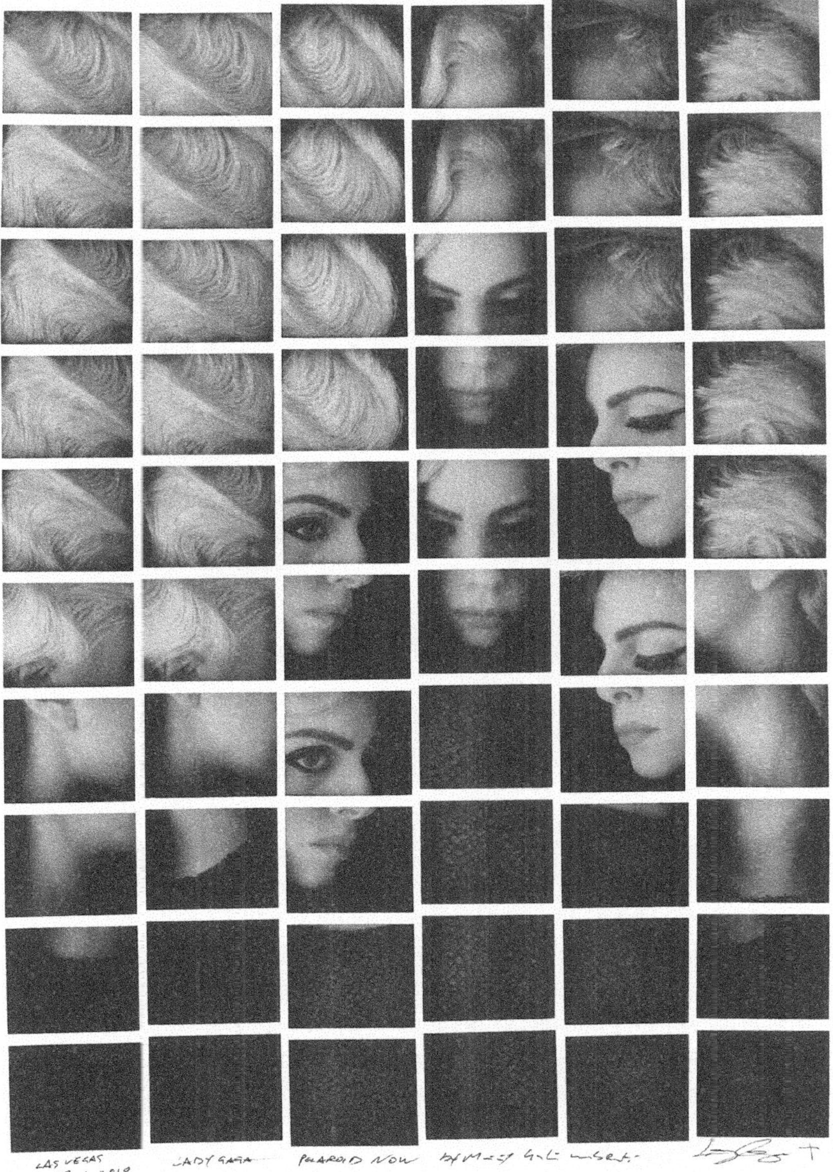

Figure 34

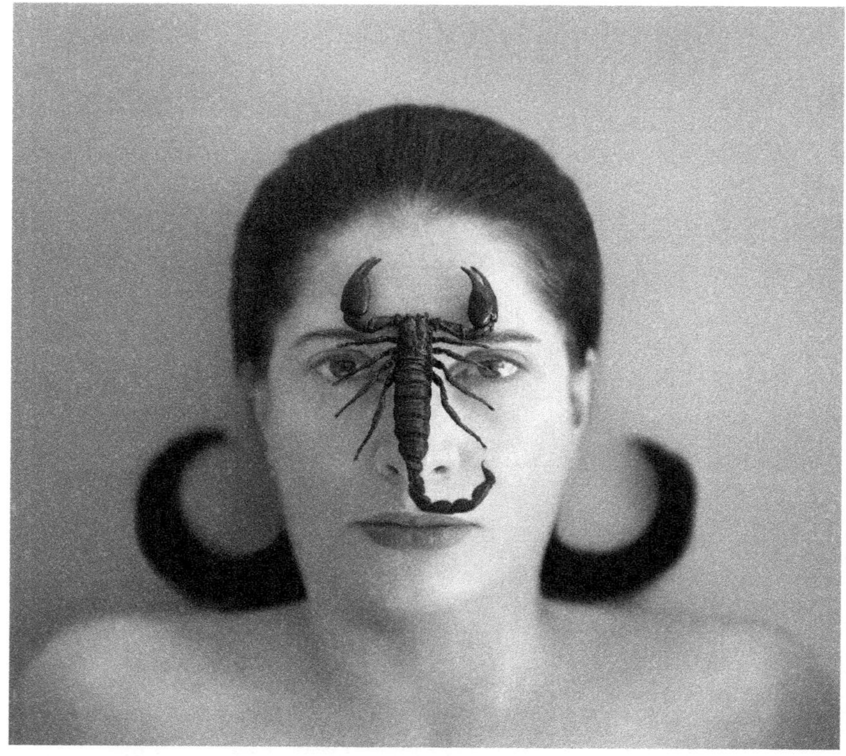

Figure 35

itself for what it is: not "something," but the irreducible "proper" of every "being," the "proper" that is "proper to" nothing nor is it the property "of" anybody, as it *is* alone in being the being that it is . . .

If the image is the presence of an absence, then the portrait, the absolute image, is the presence of the essential absence, of an absence so essential that it misplaces its proper image, sometimes makes it explode, sometimes drown, sometimes vacillate, fluster or frighten itself, but in so doing, it also beckons the inexhaustible newness of the even more other (Figure 35).

The art we call "contemporary" is not simply art from the present day. It is called "contemporary" because it inherits no form or reference: It can no longer be the art of the sacred or that of public or private glory, or that of a supposed nature or destiny of peoples. It inherits only the enigma borne by this word—*art*—that was invented at the moment when all the figures of a possible "representation" began to slip away.

It is contemporary to its own question, to its own wandering and to the always uncertain and trembling birth of forms that would be proper to being "let down" by all received properties.[2] It is contemporary to a *subject* who would be all the more *proper* in knowing itself to appear only at the moment when it disentangles itself from all properties so as to be only its proper image—but to be that image in all its truth (Figure 36).

—Translated by Sarah Clift

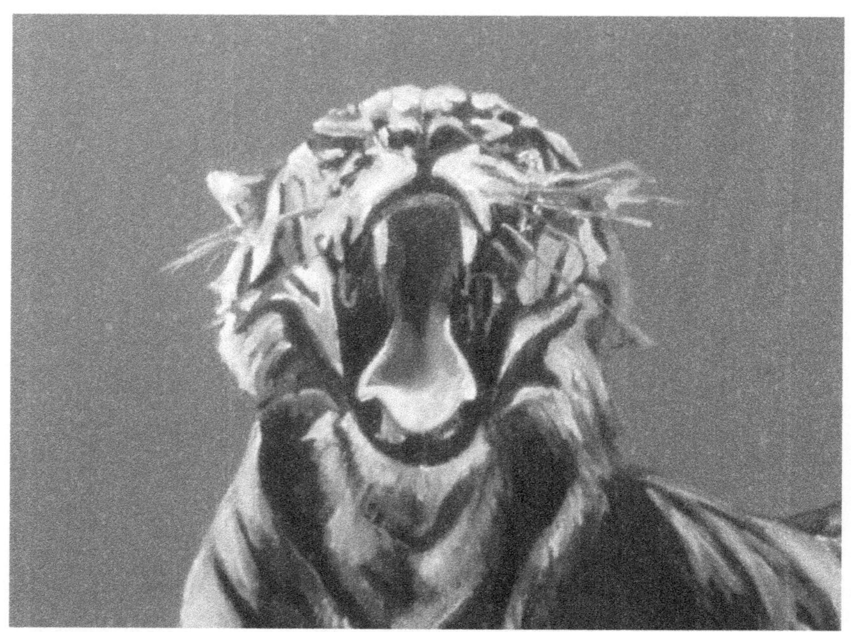

Figure 36

Notes

Introduction: The Subject of the Portrait

1. For Nancy's own extended analysis of Descartes, see *Ego Sum* (Paris: Flammarion, 1979); in English: *Ego Sum: Corpus, Anima, Fabula*, trans. Marie-Eve Morin (New York: Fordham University Press, 2016).

2. Martin Heidegger, *Prolegomena zur Geschichte des Zeitbegriffs* (Frankfurt am Main: Vittorio Klostermann, 1979) [in English: *History of the Concept of Time: Prolegomena*, trans. Theodore Kiesel (Bloomington and Indianapolis: Indiana University Press, 1985)]; and *Sein und Zeit* (Tübingen: Max Niemeyer Verlag, 1979) [in English: *Being and Time*, trans. Joan Stambaugh, foreword Dennis J. Schmidt (Albany: SUNY Press, 2010)]. For a rigorous, extended discussion of the question, see François Raffoul, *Heidegger and the Subject*, trans. David Pettigrew and Gregory Recco (Amherst, N.Y.: Humanity Books, 1998). For Heidegger's later views on Descartes and the subject in relation to the history of Being (1940), see *Nietzsche*, vol. 2 (Pfullingen: Günther Neske, 1961), 141–93.

3. See *Being and Time* for the crucial definitions of these concepts.

4. Nancy develops this relationality in connection with the simultaneous solitude of the subject in *La communauté désoeuvrée* (Paris: Christian Bourgois, 1986) [in English: *The Inoperative Community*, trans. Peter Connor et al., foreword by Christopher Fynsk (Minneapolis: University of Minnesota Press, 1991)]; Introduction to *Who Comes After the Subject?* ed. Eduardo Cadava, Peter Connor, Jean-Luc Nancy (New York and London: Routledge, 1991), 1–8; *L'être singulier pluriel* (Paris: Éditions Galilée, 1996) [in English: *Being Singular Plural*, trans. Robert D. Richardson and Anne E. O'Byrne (Stanford: Stanford University Press, 2000)]: "The question of Being and the meaning of Being has become the question of being-with and of being-together (in the sense of the world)" (35). Heidegger's political engagement for the National Socialist cause can be seen to be intimately related to his insistence on authenticity as disengagement from the crowd of the others, displaced onto the level of international and intercultural being-with (and its nationalist disavowal).

5. These writings include: *Les muses* (Paris: Éditions Galilée, 1994) [in English: *The Muses*, trans. Peggy Kamuf (Stanford: Stanford University Press, 1996)]; *À l'écoute* (Paris: Éditions Galilée, 2002) [in English: *Listening*, trans. Charlotte Mandel (New York: Fordham University Press, 2007)]; *Au fond des images* (Paris: Éditions Galilée, 2003) [in English: *The Ground of the Image*, trans. Jeff Fort (New York: Fordham University Press, 2005)]; *Nus som-

mes (La peau des images), with Frederico Ferrari (Brussels: Kliencksieck, 2006) [in English: *Being Nude (the Skin of Images)*, trans. Anne O'Byrne and Carlie Anglemire (New York: Fordham University Press, 2014)]; *Le plaisir au dessin* (Paris: Éditions Galilée, 2009) [in English: *The Pleasure in Drawing*, trans. Philip Armstrong (New York: Fordham University Press, 2013)]; and *Multiple Arts: The Muses II* (Stanford: Stanford University Press, 2006), which gathers essays by Nancy published in French in diverse contexts.

6. In the earlier book, *Corpus* (Paris: Métailié, 1992) [in English: *Corpus*, trans. Richard A. Rand (New York: Fordham University Press, 2008)], Nancy developed the notion of exposition in a section titled through the word-play "Expeausition" (31–34), as an exposition by means of the "peau" or "skin." Here, the body is existence itself as exposition, as departing from oneself toward oneself at every moment, including the self-departure into the division of the senses (33).

7. For Nancy's reflections on *poiesis*, see the first two chapters in *Multiple Arts.*

8. With these phrases, Nancy is allusively displacing Heidegger's notion that the artwork in general is the "putting (in) to (the) work of truth" (*das Ins-werk-setzen der Wahrheit*), from "Der Ursprung des Kunstwerkes" (*Holzwege* [Frankfurt am Main: Vittorio Klostermann, 1950], 1–72) [in English: "The Origin of the Work of Art," *Poetry, Language, Thought*, trans. Albert Hofstadter (New York: Harper and Row, 1971), 15–88]. Using the same phrasing further on with respect to death ("the portrait puts death itself (in) to (the) work" ["Recall"]), and glossing "death" by associating it explicitly with "finitude," "division," "eksistence," and "exposition," Nancy recalls that the finite subject always maintains a relationship also to its own death.

9. The three expressions quasi-equivalent to these in "The Other Portrait" are: reproducing, interpellating, and authority (5).

10. Cf. Jacques Lacan, *Les quatres concepts fondamentaux de la psychanalyse* (Paris: Éditions du Seuil, 1973) [in English: *Four Fundamental Concepts of Psychoanalysis*, trans. Alan Sheridan (New York: Norton, 1977)]. Some other texts in which Nancy critically analyzes, appropriates, displaces, and reflects upon Lacanian concepts include (with Philippe Lacoue-Labarthe) *Le titre de la lettre (une lecture de Lacan)* (Paris: Éditions Galilée, 1973) [in English: *The Title of the Letter: a Reading of Lacan*, trans. François Raffoul and David Pettigrew (Albany: SUNY Press, 1992)]; *À l'écoute* (English: *Listening*); *Le 'il y a' du rapport sexuel* (Paris: Éditions Galilée, 2001) [in English: "The 'There is' of the Sexual Relation" in *Corpus II: Writings on Sexuality*, trans. Anne O'Byrne (New York: Fordham University Press, 2013)].

11. In the opposition between looking and seeing in "The Look of the Subject," Nancy develops a figure of the exposition of the subject that is closely analogous to the opposition between listening and hearing in *Listening* (1ff).

12. And in this sense it is *la chose*—the "thing" and etymologically, the "cause"—which connects it once again to Lacan's analysis of the gaze as object (a) because the object (a) is frequently characterized as "the cause of desire."

13. Self-portraiture, however, does provide an image of the self-relation, and in this sense comes close to providing an image of the self. This is another sense in which Nancy claims that all portraiture tends toward self-portraiture. For one elaboration, see his detailed and astonishing reading of Johannes Gump's "Self-Portrait" in "The Look of the Portrait" below.

14. At the risk of Hegelianizing Nancy's thought on the portrait beyond his intentions (and reading history as the unfolding of structure), one might surmise that, on his account, ancient portraiture would concretize resemblance, Christian portraiture through the Reformation would instantiate recall, and modern portraiture since the seventeenth century would focus on the look.

The Look of the Portrait

The Matisse epigraph is from *Matisse: Écrits et propos sur l'art*, ed. Dominique Foucade (Paris: Hermann, 1984), 174. (My thanks to Jean-Claude Conésa.) In a note, the editor refers to the version of this remark recalled by Aragon in his own book on Matisse: "We know only these words of Rembrandt's: 'I make portraits.' In times of crisis, I have often clung to these words."

The Autonomous Portrait

1. And we could immediately add that there can be several different arts of the portrait: pictorial, sculptural, photographic, literary, musical, even choreographic. Here, however, I have limited myself to painting, in which, moreover, there are already several sorts of portrait (self/allo, simple or multiple, staged or solitary . . .). As will become clear, I am further limiting myself here to the latter, indicating on occasion how the other sorts of portrait highlight its particular traits. In art, everything is always plural, and it would thus be all the more interesting to ponder how the "portrait" is able to pick out its 'genre" from the diversity of the arts. This is merely a suggestion.

2. Jean-Marie Pontévia, *Écrits sur l'art* (Bordeaux: William Blake, 1986) 3:12. These masterly pages on the portrait, like those of Louis Marin, lie behind everything that follows.

3. With the example of Watteau's *Indifferent*, we need to make it clear that some paintings, despite appearances, need to be ruled out as portraits: Géricault's *Monomaniac of Envy* (Lyon) or Joseph Soumy's *Disdain* (Lyon, 1859), for example, as well as all other representations or stagings of affects or passions, however discreet their expression may be. (I should add that I will refer to the date and place of the paintings cited only where the works are sufficiently little-known to make this necessary.)

4. Two cases that are divided by title alone, and not the portrait; see Paul Ricoeur's "Sur un autoportrait de Rembrandt," in *Lectures 3* (Paris: Seuil, 1994). Another and far rarer sort of action would ultimately be admissible, the sort announced in the title *Portrait of a Woman Raising a Curtain* (Jean Raoux, 1720, Lyon). Here, a woman pulls up a blue curtain that, in the foreground of the painting, falls across her; she makes herself thus appear, and we could consider this gesture as a regulated transformation of the basic gesture of painting (the fabric of the canvas drawn aside in order to become a figure, the curtain raised on a presence, and so on). Doubtless it would be possible to analyze in precisely the same vein any number of portraits of reading or writing (Holbein or Quentin Metsys's *Eurasmus*), of sculptors holding a work (Titian's *Jacopo de Strada*, Vienna), or of musicians or even painters themselves holding a score or an instrument (Sofonisba Anguisscla, *Self-Portrait at the Harpsichord*, 1561, Althorp). But it goes without saying that we could extend

and refine the inquiry as well as the analysis. The "autonomous" portrait has itself various types and accents.

5. This is a position that Milan Kundera, for example, has accurately and carefully developed; see his "Le geste brutal de peintre," in *Bacon: Portraits et autoportraits* (Paris: Les Belles Lettres/Archimbault, 1996).

6. Philippe Lacoue-Labarthe has already dealt with precisely this question in *Portrait de l'artiste, en général* (Paris: Christian Bourgeois, 1979). This book—on Urs Lüthi's self-portraits—which Lacoue-Labarthe and Francois Martin followed some years later with *Retrait de l'artiste, en deux personnes* (Lyon: Éditions MEM/FRAC Rhône-Alpes, 1982), lies behind much of what is being said here, as do the studies of Pontévia and Marin. Of this question, Lacoue-Labarthe writes, among other things, that "for Baudelaire, there is something that obscurely ties these two questions to one another: that of the identity of the painting and that of the identity of the subject." This knot is the very one that I am trying to tie both anew and otherwise, having already dealt with the issue in the question of the portrait in Descartes; see Jean-Luc Nancy, *Ego Sum* (Paris: Flammarion, 1979).

7. The case of extremely large close-ups often appears contemporary, tied as it is to photography. Chuck Close, for example, with *Robert* (New York, 1974), approaches the grain of the skin—of the support and of the medium; the limit of the portrait would begin to be touched upon at the point where the figure is opened through all of its pores, even though the skin of the face, along with its other openings (nose, mouth, ears: all of the senses on offer), is obviously important for the arrangement of the look.

8. I cannot deal here with an analysis of nude portraits. The genre is well-represented in contemporary painting, particularly in self-portraits by women. See Frances Borzello, *Femmes au Miroir* (Paris: Thames and Hudson, 1988).

9. On the other hand, that the dress remain relatively discreet is a correlative requirement respected by all the best portraits. By this I mean that a good many official portraits, and so a considerable number of portraits from the classical period, have to be set to one side (albeit only slightly so); we are also dealing with the problem of defining truth in painting ... The so-called "court" portrait (later, the bourgeois portrait) often puts the function before the person (and we know how Goya shook off this genre ...); it is no longer a portrait but an emblem (one accompanied by a gesture of identification).

10. In particular, of course, the Guilds and Regents of Franz Hals, Thomas de Keyser, and others. Here again, however, the line is carefully drawn between multiple portraits (group portraits or portraits of groups) and settings that involve the action of positing some camaraderie, with all its attributes and functions ... This is why I would say that such portraits are actually quite rare.

11. We could also add double or triple portraits of the same person, in which that person does not look at him- or herself: Rigaud's *Portrait of the Artist's Mother* (Paris, 1695), for example. It is nonetheless possible, however, that the doubling of the same figure plunges or seems to plunge that figure's look into that of its double (Philippe de Champaigne, *Triple Portrait of Richelieu*); this is a variation, then, of the look plunged into our own ... On the other hand, it is no less certain that, in what used to be called "history" painting, we also find looks that are either lost in vagueness or directed upon the look of the spectator, sometimes in flagrant disregard of narrative convention; the motif of the look runs throughout the whole painting.

12. Bronzino (Berlin, 1537). This, like many of the other paintings referred to here, can be found in Norbert Schneider's *L'Art du Portrait* (Cologne: Benedikt Taschen, 1994), as well as in Flavio Caroli, *L'Anima e il Volto* (Milan: Electa, 1998).

13. For example, Moroni's *Portrait of the Duke of Albuquerque* (Berlin, 1560) or similar self-portraits by de Chirico. It is a matter of displacing the practices of the medallion (in which, it is agreed, we can see one of the origins of the portrait) and of statuary. Yet we can also see how transporting the commemorative inscription into the space of the painting displaces the functions or the senses of either and (or) each.

14. Thus Holbein's *The Basel Jurist Bonifacius Amerbach* (Basel, 1519), in which the figure itself declares, in the first person, that its art is not inferior to nature.

15. This is why the portrait was long considered to be an inferior (utilitarian) genre of painting, the noble genre being that of so-called "history painting." The documents of this history can be found in Édouard Pommier's *Théories du portrait: De la Renaissance aux Lumières* (Paris: Gallimard, 1998). One of the most striking marks of this depreciation is found in the opposition, current in Italy, between *ritarre* (to make an identity portrait, if I can put it that way) and *imitare* (to paint while correcting the real in order to perfect it). The necessity of "perfecting" or, in any case, in part redoing, embellishing, or ennobling the face that is being painted, something that has been debated throughout the entire history of the portrait, goes back as far as Aristotle, for whom good painters, "by making portraits that resemble those who are being painted, also make them more beautiful" (*Poetics* 54b8). (I am also aware of a juridical arrangement whereby Greek painters and sculptors dedicated themselves to embellishing the characters being represented; see Claudius Aelanius, *Varia historia*, mentioned by Reinhold Hohl in *Face to Face to Cyberspace*, catalogue to the exhibition of the same name [Basel: Fondation Beyler, 1999], 10.) But this supplement of "beauty" is perhaps also what completes the spiritual or moral "resemblance," perhaps even what completes "resemblance" as a whole by disengaging the subject's "own" traits for themselves. In this regard, see the commentaries on Aristotle's remarks in Roselyne Dupont-Roc and Jean Lallot's edition of the *Poetics* (Paris: Seuil, 1980).

16. "The face of the other is his way of signifying," writes Emmanuel Levinas in *Altérité et Transcendance* (Montpellier: Fata Morgana, 1995), 172.

17. Pommier, *Théories du portrait*, 55. The translation adopted by Pommier rather displaces, and wrongly, in my view, the accent of the first sentence. It would be necessary to follow how the relation of the face to the soul or the spirit has been progressively modified alongside the history of the portrait: From "mirror of the soul," the face became a mere effect of the agitation of the passions (an idea developed by Le Brun) before the risky adventures of the "physiognomies" of the eighteenth century and the various characterologies and typologies of the nineteenth (in which the portrait gets lost in classificatory identification, something to which photography is often thought to be in thrall). See Jean-Jacques Courtine and Claudine Haroche, *Histoire du visage* (Paris: Rivages, 1984 and 1988).

18. See Jacques Derrida, "Forcener le subjectile," in *Artaud. Dessins et portraits* (Paris: Gallimard, 1986), which speaks of nothing other than an unidentifiable identity between the subject and the support of painting.

19. G. W. F. Hegel, *Asthetik, in Werke in zwanzig Bände*, ed. Eva Moldenhauer and Michael Karl Markus (Frankfurt am Main: Suhrkamp, 1971), vol. 13, 3.iii.1 §2c Let me take

this opportunity to recall that, in French, the word *portrait* denoted, first and foremost, the whole of painting (see Villard de Honnecourt's *Livre de portraiture* of the thirteenth century, which contains models for all sorts of scenarios. The modern usage of the term comes into play only with Félibien).

20. This contradictory imitation obviously belongs to the problematic developed at length by Lacoue-Labarthe on the subject of an "originary" *mimesis*, something to which he had already made reference in his study of the self-portrait.

21. Because I shall want to come back later on to the look of the portrait, let us here simply pose the following question: Why doesn't Hegel speak of this look when he evokes the painting of the face (of the face "shaped by the labor of Spirit" that is thus itself already an artistic work . . .)? And we should remember that it is Hegel who declares elsewhere that art transforms every phenomenon into a look: "art makes each one of its works into a thousand-eyed Argus in which the inner soul and Spirit is seen at every point" (*Werke*, vol. 13, 1.iii.A §1; translated by T. M. Knox as *Aesthetics* [Oxford University Press, 1975], 153–54). And it is Hegel, too, who never fails to mention the absence of the look in statuary. So why this singular forgetting? Without wanting to belabor the point, given the brevity of the passage on the portrait, let me put forward the hypothesis that he unconsciously refuses to accord too much "spirituality" to painting in order to ensure its place on the side of music and poetry, in which the "sensible" tends to be dissolved. Moreover, although he does indeed recognize "spiritual life" in painting, in the remarks that precede and immediately follow this passage, Hegel still prefers to try to find that "spiritual life" in decidedly religious themes (Madonna and Christ, figures of whom there could precisely be no portrait, or at least no portrait that could present itself as such).

22. "Every painter paints himself," a phrase attributed to Cosimo de Medici. See Pontévia, *Écrits sur l'art*, 38.

23. Doubtless this essay touches closely on questions connected to Heidegger's idea of art as a putting (in) to (the) work of truth, something that also involves a setting to one side of the mimetic or representational conception of art, a conception whose acme the portrait might well be seen to be. (Nonetheless, Heidegger still seems to find no use whatsoever for the portrait, despite the references in the *Kantbuch* to the death mask and even to photographs of death masks; as we shall see, these have precisely nothing in common, however.) Here, I shall not embark on an analysis that still needs to be opened up.

24. These three moments are logical or dialectical: The look will assume or sublate the others; in a sense, however, they also have a certain historical relevance: We could show how the accent has successively shifted from the fifteenth century to our own day, and we could presumably also find in them a certain topical or taxonomic value as regards the different genres of portraits (although I'm not claiming to speak about all forms of the portrait, simply the ones I'm looking at here). But it goes without saying that they are also three simultaneous and indivisible traits of the portrait itself.

Resemblance

1. The phrase articulates the desire for an integral representation while also expressing what matters to painting: the fact that its subject does not speak, *that is, the fact that its subject speaks through painting alone, and all it says is "ego sum"* . . . On the frequency of this

phrase and on the debates surrounding the dignity of the portrait, see Pommier, *Théories du portrait*. In terms of resemblance in its individual precision, we would need to trace how, in the Renaissance, it came to succeed, by opposing the aspects of conventional typology still attached to the earliest portraits. What is remarkable about the portrait is that it can only be opposed to the idea of a *type* and so, in this sense, of a *model* (whether it be the model of sanctity, of divinity, of virtue or vice, of character or function, etc., whatever). Enrico Castelnuovo has drawn attention to the move from the "typical" portrait (an idea tied to the notion of the medallion) to the "authentic" portrait. A little later on, however, there would be different *types of portraits*: the court portrait, the moral portrait, portraits "in painting" (itself another sort of portrait), etc. On this, see *Visages du grand siècle* (Paris: Somogy, 1997).

2. One could devote an entire study to the frequency and the (precisely) typical character of stories of recognition through portraits, of blinding flashes of insight before and for portraits, etc., in both historical and fictional narratives from the Renaissance to the eighteenth century. These sorts of scenes are sometimes represented, often being set way back inside a portrait such as Rubens's *Henry IV Admiring a Portrait of Maria de Medici* (Louvre). In *The Magic Flute*, Pamino exclaims, "This portrait is of an entrancing beauty."

3. The question of the portrait's and the self-portrait's reference, a question that I will have to address from several angles, has been raised in Jean-Louis Déotté, Éric Van de Casteele, and Michel Servière's *Portrait, autoportrait* (Paris: Osiris, 1987), among other works. Let us hold on to the following powerful remarks made by Servière: "If we paint, paint ourselves, we do so in order to unpaint, to unmake and remake ourselves. A solitary injunction: junk, abandon the model" (110).

4. Complete references to the works that appear in the text are found at the end of Portrait in the "List of Figures." The creators and the titles of some of them already appear in the text; in cases where what is at issue is the image alone, the references can be consulted afterward.

5. The self-portrait with mirror is both frequent and old. The first ones we know of are those of Marcia, who painted two miniatures (1402 and 1404). See the images and texts in Borzello, *Femmes au miroir*, 19–21.

6. "Verso il riguardante," says Roberto Contini in Caroli, *L'Anima e il Volto*, 284.

7. I owe this valuable insight to Sergio Risaliti.

8. As suggested by Contini's remarks in Caroli's *L'Anima e il Volto*. Still, I regret not knowing how to interpret the gilded cord to the left of the cat.

9. Something abundantly illustrated in "vanity" paintings, in certain "toilettes" etc. We would have to study all the associations made in painting between the portrait and the mirror and the uses of the mirror itself, as well as various connections between this theme and those of Narcissus, Sosia, and the double in general: This entire family of motifs displays essential differences regarding the problematic of the portrait.

10. Such, in fact, would be the case with any "self-portrait." We could also consider the more developed version of this representation of the representation of the self in, say, Norman Rockwell's ironic *Self-Portrait* (cover of *The Post*, February 13, 1960), which features several famous self-portraits as well as the painter's own image in the mirror and on canvas with and without eyes and/or glasses, etc. (the painting is mentioned by Déotté, Van de Casteele, and Servière in *Portrait, autoportrait*). We can compare this work to

Rockwell's own *Mirror*, which concentrates all the signs of narcissism. With this genre of representation, however, we leave painting behind, not because the intention is humorous but because the humor stems from a signifying excess (something from which Gumpp's self-portrait is not wholly exempt).

11. For any portrait, whether or not it chooses to call itself one, it is wholly impossible to decide whether or not it is painted after a single model or multiple models, or indeed after any model at all, on the basis of the painting alone.

12. In the sixteenth century, the word "resemblance" had the sense of "portrait," in the expression *ressemblance faite sur le vif*, for example. We should also note the fact that "resemblance" differs from "reproduction" or from "copy" with regard to the value of approximation. It is only "semblance" that "resembles," that is an "allure," an "air," or an "aspect." In point of fact, all the portrait ever does is manifest approximate allures of absence. *Resemblance turns on its own absence*: and to turn thus is, strictly speaking, the gesture of the painter's hand.

13. Auguste Pellerin was a great collector and seller of paintings.

14. The same setup is employed in the 1916 portrait.

15. Or *extracting* [traire]: "bringing out." Such is the emblematic value of the trace or the trait. The trace of the trait is, first and foremost, what is ex-tracted [*ex-trait*]. Painting is the extraction of the trace or the trait. The "por-" of "portray," homonymous with the French *pour*, "for," is an intensifier (like the "re-" of "representing" or "resembling"). Just as *repraesentatio* (which follows *praesentatio*) is a putting forward, a bringing to presence, so to portray is to draw forward, to draw out, to present everything. It is to *render* present. To portray is to draw out presence—even if the presence in question is only that of an absence.

16. Hence the pleasure taken in *mimesis*, according to Aristotle's well-known formulation. It is not the pleasure of repetition but the pleasure of coming to light and extraction (although, if you prefer, the two are strictly indiscernible).

17. There is a whole typology to be drawn of mouths in portraits; a little later, I shall want to turn to the half-open mouth of Lotto's *Young Man*. Here, for the moment, is what Schelling has to say: "In this way, the formative arts are only the dead word, and yet they are still *words*, still the act of speaking; the more completely this speaking dies—as great as the utterance that turns to stone on Niobe's lips—the more sublime is art in its own fashion." F. W. J. Schelling, *Sämtliche Werke*, ed. K. F. A. Schelling (Stuttgart: J. G. Cotta, 1860); translated by D. W. Stott as *The Philosophy of Art* (Minneapolis: University of Minnesota Press, 1989), 101.

Recall

1. Whence the numerous profile portraits in the portrait's early years (often a device used to hide a flaw in the face, as in the case of the famous Federigo da Montefeltre, whose left profile only was painted by Piero della Francesca [Florence] because the right side was missing an eye). Whence, too, the portraits in which the figure holds a medallion. We would also need to trace the history of the progressive move to portraits of people of less elevated status (initially proscribed) and thence to unflattering portraits of elevated figures (see Goya).

2. The phrase is from the valuable book by Jean-Christophe Bailly cited previously. It is interesting to note that portraits explicitly connected to death (with the skull, for example in the various Vanities or Madeleines) are not quite so numerous, despite some truly remarkable cases in Holbein (*The Ambassadors*), Lovis Corinth, Picasso, and Barceló, and in Antonio Saura's *Self-Portrait* (1989), which, for all intents and purposes, is the self-portrait of the head of a dead man. Most of the time, however, it is as if death (infinite absence) had no need of being the theme of portraits because its presence or substance (its subjectivity) is already marked within the portrait as a whole.

3. "Do not hide your face from me; that I die—so as not to die—but that I may see it . . .! you, the height of form, who forms everything [*formosissime*]" (St. Augustine, *Confessions* 1.5.12). *Formosissime*: the most formed and the most beautiful, beauty being the correlate of form and form the completion of presence.

4. Of course, there have been plenty of hypotheses, although no firm conclusions. See Wendy Stedman Sheard, "Les Portraits," in *Lorenzo Lotto* (Paris: Réunion des Musées Nationaux, 1998), 44, notes and bibliography.

5. Many similar figures offer their very reserve and self-absorption in this way: Titian's *Man With Grey Eyes* (Florence), Giacometti's *Caroline* (Basel), Picasso's *Olga Koklowa* (1917, Marina Picasso Collection), Memling's *Portrait of a Man* (The Hague), *Ada in White Dress* by Alex Katz (1958, Robert Miller Gallery), Soutine's *Homage to Marie Lecomte* (private collection; see Caroli, *L'Anima e il Volto*, 495): a quick list that has no other aim than to evoke the endless "et cetera" that is, in short, one of the major expressions of the portrait, if we can indeed speak here of an "expression" and not, rather better, of an inexpression in which the *recall to intimacy* is unmistakably impressed.

6. Allow me to refer to two other texts: "L'Image—le distinct," in the catalogue to the "Heaven" exhibition (Düsseldorf Kunsthalle, Summer 1999), and "L'Immémorial," in *Cet objet . . .* (Nancy: École nationale des Beaux-Arts, 1999).

7. We could easily show this in the case of court portraits.

8. To his portrait of a child, *Sigismondo Ponzone* (Cremona), Genovesino adds this inscription: "Father, you who have taken part in my formation, receive me formed anew by art."

9. Dürer, as we know, painted himself in the guise of Christ. The theology of man "in the image of God" and that of the Son as the "visible image of the visible" (Paul), the Incarnation and Transubstantiation, together constitute, in the self-deconstruction that Christianity releases onto itself, the armature of every theory of the subject and the easel of all portraiture.

10. Of course, the real movement is more complex. Monologotheism was a long time coming. When Plotinus says that Phidias represented Zeus such as he would be were he to want to appear (*Enneads* 5.8.1), we are on the verge of a transition between a divinity that moves toward presence and one that flies from it. From Plato to Plotinus, the whole of philosophy is played out around a (non)resemblance of and to the "Good."

11. That is, both the prohibition on staying with any vision whatsoever, even that of the sky and light, before that of and in God (see, for example, Deuteronomy 40 66), and the prohibition on reproducing God's formative gesture (Koran 40:66, for example); this is the figure without figure of the figuration of everything that remains out of reach. The history of Western art has constantly been stretched by the (a)theology of an arche-artistic god.

12. Didn't Pope John Paul II feel the need to remind us that God the father ought not to be represented as an old man with a beard? The questions concerning the representation of God, of the impossibility of painting a "portrait" of Christ, etc., were regulated centuries ago, by Catholicism itself, in much the same way as the constant depiction of the Spirit by a bird or by a light, and only very rarely by a human face. We might say that the portrait has taken over from Spirit, leaving the Father and the Son, like Mary, a sort of figuration without portraiture (which again underlines the importance of the declaration: a Madonna can be a portrait, and has been so more than once, but not avowedly so, not distinguished as such. It is still the case that the painting of a Madonna or a Helen or a Venus is organized somewhat differently, however slight such a difference may be, than a painting orchestrated strictly "around a figure").

13. In the broad sense in which I am here using the term, which includes a large percentage of Western figures up to Giotto.

14. As Origen says, after Paul, *Peri Archon* 1.2.6. On the move from the icon to the portrait, see the valuable history provided by Hans Belting in *Image et Culte* (Paris: Cerf, 1998).

Look

1. It has recently been shown, by means of statistics drawn from thousands of portraits, that the vertical median axis of the painting most often passes through one of the eyes. Still, the look comes not from the eyes alone but equally from the mouth (very often central), the nostrils, and the ears, from each of the pores and touches of paint. Giacometti: "If I have the curve of the eye, I also have its orbit; if I have the orbit, I have the root of the nose, I have the point of the nose, I have the holes of the nose, I have the mouth." See the conversation with Jacques Dupin in Ernst Scheidegger and Peter Münger's 1965 film *Alberto Giacometti*, cited in Hohl, *Face to Face to Cyberspace*.

2. We would have to analyze more closely the technical ingenuity employed in capturing the resemblance of the look, the gleam of the eye and the light that reflects in it so as to shine out of it. Vinci invented the technique of using a third point of light to complete the two-point arrangement that had been used before him to render the light of the eye. Still, it would also be necessary to consider how the look only looks with the contours of the face as a whole, of the mouth and the cheekbones, the nostrils, and the ears . . . Along with the face and its whole aspect, the look puts into play the whole of sense, of the ability to be affected and to be touched. In modern times, it is more and more the openness of the eye, a black opacity of an emptying, that will have guided the (re)semblance of the look. The fact that the look is what is proper to painting, its subject, is illustrated by the technique of Bernin, who, in order to complete a bust of the king, sketched out the eye on the stone itself. (My thanks to Stefano Chiodi on this point.)

3. Giulio Paolini has reproduced another of Lotto's portraits, another *Young Man*, from the same period (Florence), giving it the title *Giovane che guarda Lorenzo Lotto* (1967, artist's collection). In 1981, the same young man, his look slightly shifted, was given the title *Contrafigura (critica del punti di vista)* (reproduced in *Giulio Paolini. Images* [Villeurbanne: Le Nouveau Musée, 1984]), and can be compared to other works by the same artist around portraits by Poussin or Ingres, for example. (My thanks to Jean-Claude Conésa.) Barceló

writes: "I often work with a blind man ... When painting a portrait there s something that can't be avoided, the model's look.... With a blind man, there's a sort of *marvelous impunity* that allows me to avoid this fear of the look" (*Miguel Barceló* [Paris Éditions du Jeu de Paume / Réunion des Musées Nationaux, 1996], 128).

4. To take just two of the numerous examples available to us, Rogier van der Weyden, *Portrait of a Woman* (circa 1460, Washington) and Renato Guttuso, *Mimise col cappello rosso* (1940, Verona). More rarely, the look is almost closed, absent, or empty (reduced to a black hole): Holbein the Younger, *Erasmus in profile* (1523, Louvre); Picasso, *Self-Portrait* (1983, private collection) Monet, *Camille sur la plage* (1870, Paris); Modigliani, *Portrait of Jeanne Hebitène* and so on.

5. It turns toward me, stares at me, and concerns me; it is my business, and, as we say, "it only has eyes for me."

6. The painting comes from an African journey (on the back, the artist has painted the words "Two papayas").

7. *Decet, decorum.*

8. Ludwig Wittgenstein, *Remarks on the Philosophy of Psychology*, ed. and trans. G. E. M. Anscobe and G. H. von Wright (Oxford: Blackwell, 1980), vol. 1: §1100. [Nancy, citing Gérard Granel's translation, reads Wittgenstein's *Blick* as *regard* ("look").—Trans.]

9. Here, we would need to take up the analysis of the "encounter" in Duchamp's ready-mades. I refer to the analyses of Thierry de Duve and to the work in progress by Tomàs Maïa.

10. See Jean-Pierre Raynaud's *Self-Portrait (I)* (Osaka, 1980), a sculpture that has no other "figure" than the shapes from which it is formed. On the look in Picasso, let me take the following remark from Françoise Gilot, one of thousands of available references: "When he met us, he saw in Geneviève a perfection of forms and, in me, a disquiet that echoes his own character. And, for him, this contrast became an image.... He said somewhere: 'I encounter beings that I painted twenty years ago.'" Cited by Rosalind Krauss, "Vivre avec Picasso," in *Je suis le cahier. Les Carnets de Picasso* (Paris: Grasset/Fasquelle, 1986), 121. On Giacometti, see Reinhold Hohl's essays "Das blickende Bildnis," in Hohl, *Face to Face to Cyberspace*; and "Giacometti ou l'autoportrait-défi," in Joëlle Moulin *Autoportraits du XXe siècle* (Paris: Adam Biro, 1999). See, too, Jean Genet's *L'Atelier d'Alberto Giacometti* (Décines: Barbezat, 1963). Bacon declares, "with faces, you have to capture the energy that emanates from them." (quoted in Hohl, *Face to Face to Cyberspace*, 71). For examples of hyperrealist portraits, see in particular the work of Chuck Close and Franz Gertsch; see also the texts and documents in Dubuffet.

L'altro ritratto

1. Cristiana Collu, director of the Museo di Arte Moderna e Contemporanea di Rovereto e Trento, entrusted me with curating an exhibition of the same name, held at Rovereto from October 2013 to January 2014. This text is also meant to express my gratitude for the confidence she had in me, and for the chance to take on this project. The first version appeared in Italian for the exhibition catalogue (*L'Altro Ritratto*, Italian trans. M. Villani, Naples: Rovereto, MART, 2013).

2. See, for example, *Le Pourtraict de la santé où est au vif representée la Reigle universelle et particuliere, de bien sainement et longuement vivre* by Joseph Du Chesne (1546–1609).

3. In another context, one could extend this analysis to include many other languages.

4. Jean-Christophe Bailly, *Le Champ mimétique* (Paris: Le Seuil, 2005), 45.

5. See Jean-Christophe Bailly, *L'Apostrophe muette* (Paris: Hazan, 1997). Bailly practices a historical hermeneutic in this work that is quite different from the one I am attempting here, but the two do not contradict each other.

6. On this point, we need to recall Heidegger's famous analysis in his *Kantbuch* and Blanchot's in *L'Espace littéraire*, as well as the many reflections on the portrait found throughout his *récits* and other texts.

Character

1. We will have occasion later on to return to the various postures used in portraiture: profile (seen from the front or from behind), facing, bust or whole body, three-quarters . . . indeed, from the back (such as Pliny the Elder describes it in the context of a portrait of Hercules by Apelles, a very long time before contemporary artists began using this about-face). This paragon of representation also seems to aim at complicating or even at frustrating the desire for a simple and obvious likeness.

The Eye

1. My text "The Look of the Portrait," included in this volume, is devoted to the look as the very origin of the portrait.

2. Charles Baudelaire, *The Love of Lies*, the title of which clearly indicates the subject: the dishonesty of seduction and the pleasure of giving in to it. If the look of one portrait attracts more than another, it is because it misleads—but it does so by manifesting the irresistible and infinite attraction that one expects of a look.

Visageity

1. J.-L. Schefer, *Figure peintes*, 145. Reference must also be made here to the book by Georges Didi-Huberman, *Ce que nous voyons, ce qui nous regarde* (Paris: Minuit, 1992).

Mimesis

1. See Plato, *Sophist* in *The Collected dialogues.* ed. Edith Hamilton and Huntington Cairns (New Jersey: Princeton University Press, 1961), 267a. ff.

2. Of the body, and thus necessarily of the face, because the deliberate representation of a headless body is not really possible or even imaginable—except for the representation of a torture—before relatively recent times.

3. Or of the East, because the Chinese tradition offers reflections on the question of the portrait that are not foreign to those of the West (see note in "Ipseity" in this volume). The Indian tradition should also be revisited in this regard. Regarding ancient Egypt, one finds mimetic aspects mixed with "archetypal" or "hierophantic" ones.

Withdrawn Presence

1. As we recalled earlier, this is also the case for Socrates in the *Sophist*.

2. Aristotle, *Poetics* in *The Complete Works of Aristotle.* Volume II, ed. Jonathan Barnes (New Jersey: Princeton University Press, 1984), 1448b. ff.

3. That is, the presentation to a subject.

4. See Jacques Derrida et al., *Mimesis des articulations* (Paris: Aubier-Flammarion, 1975). Aside from this particular work, there are numerous developments of the question of "mimesis" in Derrida and even more emphatically in the work of Philippe Lacoue-Labarthe, whose thinking about "mimesis without model" resonates strongly here.

5. Levinas achives a kind of excess by reversing the terms of visual art when he gives the name of "face" to the invisible that he designates as the "Other."

6. "*Interior intimo meo, superior summon meo,*" Augustine, *Confessions,* trans. Henry Chadwick (Oxford: Oxford University Press, 1991), 43.

Ipseity

1. As we've seen, and as we shall continue to see, the problematic of the portrait cannot be dissociated from its developments, complications, and displacements along the course of a history. This history is above all Western, and even in a sense that keeps its distance from the orthodox icon, the sacred character of which eludes questions of representation. The history of the portrait in Chinese art has provoked just as many comparable considerations as those of the West regarding the distinction between the reproduction of visible traits and the transmission, notably through the look, of a "spirit.' On this point, see Hubert Delahaye, "Faire un portrait" in *Etudes chinoises*, vol. XII, nos. 1–2, Spring–Fall, 1994).

2. Jacques Derrida, *Memoirs of the Blind,* trans. Pascale-Anne Brault and Michael Naas (Chicago: University of Chicago Press, 1993).

Theophary

1. On this self-portrait, see Hans Belting's analysis in *Das echte Bild* (Munich: C. H. Beck, 2006).

2. See Hans Belting, *Das echte Bild*, chapter IV.

Revelation

1. On this work, see Philippe Lacoue-Labarthe, *Portrait de l'artiste en général* (Paris: Christian Bourgois, 1979).

2. This is the title of the work by Hans Belting cited earlier, *Das echte Bild* [The Genuine Image].

3. See also the famous ending of Michel Foucault's *The Order of Things*.

4. Here one could drift toward the theme of veiled/unveiled images and the active, contagious, threatening, and well-known power attributed to images by a long-standing and still lively tradition. See also the formulation noted by da Vinci that says to a veiled

image: "Do not unveil if liberty is precious to you; my face is the prison of love," cited here from Horst Bredekamp, *Theorie des Bildakts* (Berlin: Suhrkamp, 2010), 17. Bredekamp's work contains exceedingly rich material on the subject of the active powers of the image and in particular of its look.

5. Charles Baudelaire, *Paris Spleen, 1869*, trans. Louis Varèse (New York: New Directions Books, 1970), 46.

Divine Abandonment

1. We are referring here to the section on Cézanne in Eric Alliez, in collaboration with Jean-Clet Martin, *L'Œil-cerveau—nouvelles histoires de la peinture moderne* (Paris: Vrin, 2007), 415ff.

2. It is remarkable that photography, "inscription of light," which was initially received as a new mode of the "genuine image," in fact performed very quickly less as a means of recording than as a construction of space and of light.

Dis-figuration

1. See Sigmund Freud, "A Difficulty in the Path of Psychoanalysis" (1917), *The Complete Psychological Works of Sigmund Freud*, vol. XVII, ed. James Strachey (London: Vintage Books, 2001), 135–44.

2. Georges Bataille, "Human Face," trans. Annette Michelson, *October* 36 (1986): 17–21. Bataille's essay plays a central role in Georges Didi-Huberman's *La Ressemblance informe ou le gai savoir visuel selon Georges Bataille* (Paris: Macula, 1995), the title and content of which are particularly relevant to our subject.

3. Didi-Huberman, *La Ressemblance informe . . .* , 167ff.

4. Ibid., 167.

5. Alain Buisine, "L'indéfigurable même" in *Le Portrait dans l'art contemporain—1945–1992* (the catalogue for an exhibition of the same name, organized by the Musée d'art moderne et d'art contemporain of Nice in 1992), 36. This catalogue is an excellent reference work for the period in question.

Eclipse

1. Of course, and despite the indication given above regarding the turn of the twentieth to the twenty-first centuries, there can be no question of a simple historical succession. Everything begins and everything continues before and after the bearings that must remain approximate.

2. See Erwin Panofsky's book of the same name, *Idea: A Concept in Art Theory*, trans. Joseph J. S. Peake (Columbia: University of South Carolina Press, 1968).

3. J. L. Schefer, *Figures Peintes*, 321. What follows here on the subject of narcissism is also indebted to this part of the book.

4. In *Art absolument* 8, Spring 2004, 54.

Infinite Detachment

1. Martin Heidegger, *Being and Time*, trans. Joan Stambaugh (Albany: SUNY Press, 1996), § 38. Here, I leave aside all necessary analyses of this passage; I presented some of them in "The Decision of Existence" in *The Birth to Presence*, trans. Brian Holmes (Stanford: Stanford University Press, 1993).

2. Max Imdahl, *Reflexion Theorie Methode* (Frankfurt: Suhrkamp, 1996), 418.

3. See Philippe Lacoue-Labarthe, *La Vraie Semblance* (Paris: Galilée, 2008).

4. The images of what Georges Didi-Huberman calls "exposed peoples, exposing peoples" also belong to this category. See Georges Didi-Huberman, *Peuples exposés, peuples exposants* (Paris: Minuit, 2013).

5. Alfonso Cariolato, "Figure, aspect, rythme" in *La Figure dans l'art* (Antibes: Musée Picasso/Bordeaux, William Blake & Co., 2005), 70.

6. This *Narciso* by Oscar Muñoz is a portrait traced in coal on the water in a sink. It disappears down the drain once the plug is pulled.

Coda I

1. Jean-Christophe Bailly, *Le Champ mimétique*, 45.

2. Yves Bonnefoy, *Remarques sur le regard* (Paris: Calmann-Lévy, 2002), 122. Here Bonnefoy is opposing Giacometti to Picasso who, he writes, "was afraid, in painting in any case, of returning his looks" because, if he had had the chance to do Giacometti's portrait, "once immobilized, [the latter] would have stared at him unrelentingly." In an opposite sense, Giacometti doubtless had no desire to do Picasso's portrait, being repelled by "confronting a look so skeptical, so lively, and so rapid—the look of a predator—that it would not have allowed itself to be captured by the trance . . ."

3. Maurice Merleau-Ponty, "A Note on Machiavelli," *Signs*, trans. Richard C. McCleary (Evanston: Northwestern University Press, 1964), 212.

Coda III

1. Michel Guérin, *La Peinture effarée* (Paris: La Transparence, 2011), 59.

2. One could also say proper to a lack of character in all the characters and all the characteristics we might have at our disposal, but a lack by virtue of which a stronger truth is affirmed than that of typologies and heroic figures. I am alluding here to a work by Jérôme Lèbre, *Les Caractères impossibles* (Paris: Bayard, 2014).

Figures

Figure 12. Albrecht Dürer, *Self-portrait in fur cloak* (1500). Oil on board, 48.9 × 67.1 cm. Bpk Bildagentur / Alte Pinakothek, Bayerische Staatsgemaeldesammlungen, Munich, Germany. Art Resource, N.Y.

Figure 13. Rembrandt Harmensz van Rijn, *Self-portrait, wearing a White Feathered Bonnet*. Oil painting on lime or poplar panel. Buckland Abbey, Devon, Great Britain. National Trust Photo Library / Art Resource, N.Y.

Figure 14. Urs Lüthi, *Lüthi Also Cries For You* (1970). Courtesy of the artist.

Figure 15. Paul Cézanne, *Self Portrait with Palette*. Oil on canvas. Foundation E. G. Buehrle, Zurich, Switzerland. Erich Lessing / Art Resource, N.Y.

Figure 16. Joan Miró, Joan, *Self-portrait* (1960). Oil on canvas, 146.5 × 96.9 cm. Fundacion Joan Miro, Barcelona, Spain. Album / Art Resource, N.Y. © Successió Miró / Artists Rights Society (ARS), New York / ADAGP, Paris 2018.

Figure 17. Piet Mondrian, *Self-portrait* (1918), Haags Gemeentemuseum, The Hague, The Netherlands. Cameraphoto Arte, Venice / Art Resource, N.Y.

Figure 18. Marcel Duchamp, *Yvonne and Magdeleine Torn in Tatters* (1911). Oil on canvas. 23¾ × 287/8 inches. The Louise and Walter Arensberg Collection, 1950. The Philadelphia Museum of Art / Art Resource, N.Y. © Association Marcel Duchamp / ADAGP, Paris / Artists Rights Society (ARS), New York 2018.

Figure 19. Jean Fautrier, *Hostage Head* (1945). Oil on paper, remount, 35 × 27 cm. Musee National d'Art Moderne, Centre Georges Pompidou, Paris © CNAC / MNAM / Dist. RMN-Grand Palais / Art Resource, N.Y.

Figure 20. Jackson Pollock, *Portrait and a Dream* (1953). Oil and enamel on canvas, 58½ × 134¾ in. Dallas Museum of Art, gift of Mr. and Mrs. Algur H. Meadows and the Meadows Foundation, Incorporated 1967.8. © 2018 The Pollock-Krasner Foundation / Artists Rights Society (ARS), New York.

Figure 21. Erwin Olaf, *Margaret Portrait* (from the series *Grief*, 2007). Courtesy of Flatland Gallery, Amsterdam, The Netherlands.

Figure 22. Marc Quinn, *Self* (1991). Blood (artist's), stainless steel, Perspex, and refrigeration equipment. 208 × 63 × 63 cm. Courtesy of Marc Quinn studio. Photo by Marc Quinn studio.

Figure 23. Rineke Dijkstra, *Ruth Drawing Picasso* (2009). Single-channel HD video-installation with sound, 6 min. 33 sec., looped. © Rineke Dijkstra.

Figure 24. Aziz + Cucher, *Rick* (*Dystopia* series, 1994). Courtesy of Aziz and Cucher.

Figure 25. David Hockney, *Portrait of Nick Wilder* (1996). Acrylic on canvas. 72 × 72 in. © David Hockney.

Figure 26. Mitchell Grafton, *Girl with the Pearl Earring Selfie* (after Vermeer). Used by permission of Mitchell Grafton, Panama City, Florida.

Figure 27. Oscar Muñoz, *Narciso* (2001–2002).

Figure 28. Curiosity (Mars Rover), *Self-portrait* (October 31, 2012). Courtesy of NASA / JPL-Caltech / MSSS, via NASA Mars Exploration.

Figure 29. Tony Bevan, *Self-Portrait PC1218* (2012). © 2018 Artists Rights Society (ARS), New York / DACS, London.

Figure 30. Mathilde Hiesse, *Untitled* (2009).

Figure 31. Marc Quinn, *Cloned DNA Self Portrait, 26.09.01* (2001). Stainless steel, polycarbonate agar jelly, bacteria colonies, cloned human DNA. 26.2 × 20.5 × 2.7 cm. Photo: Stephen White, courtesy White Cube, London.

Figure 32. Jonathon Keats, *Cloning Celebrity: Gaga and Obama* (2012). Courtesy of the artist.

Figure 33. Louise Bourgeois, *Self-Portrait (Untitled)* (1942). Ink on squared paper, 28.0 × 21.5 cm. Musee National d'Art Moderne, Centre Georges Pompidou, Paris © CNAC / MNAM / Dist. RMN-Grand Palais / Art Resource, N.Y. Photo: Zindman Fremont, © The Easton Foundation / Licensed by VAGA, N.Y.

Figure 34. Maurizio Galimberti, *Lady Gaga* (2010). Courtesy of the artist.

Figure 35. Marina Abramović, *Portrait with Scorpion (Open Eyes)* (2005). Silver Gelatin Print. © 2018 Marina Abramović. Courtesy of Sean Kelly Gallery / (ARS), New York.

Figure 36. Jacques Monory, Detail from *Tiger n° 5* (2008). Oil on canvas, 320 × 380 cm. Collection Fondation Maeght. © 2018 Artists Rights Society (ARS), New York / ADAGP, Paris.

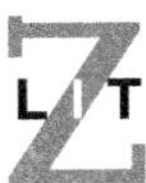 Sara Guyer and Brian McGrath, series editors

Sara Guyer, *Reading with John Clare: Biopoetics, Sovereignty, Romanticism*.

Philippe Lacoue-Labarthe, *Ending and Unending Agony: On Maurice Blanchot*. Translated by Hannes Opelz.

Emily Rohrbach, *Modernity's Mist: British Romanticism and the Poetics of Anticipation*.

Marc Redfield, *Theory at Yale: The Strange Case of Deconstruction in America*.

Jacques Khalip and Forest Pyle (eds.), *Constellations of a Contemporary Romanticism*.

Geoffrey Bennington, *Kant on the Frontier: Philosophy, Politics, and the Ends of the Earth*.

Frédéric Neyrat, *Atopias: Manifesto for a Radical Existentialism*. Translated by Walt Hunter and Lindsay Turner, Foreword by Steven Shaviro.

Jacques Khalip, *Last Things: Disastrous Form from Kant to Hujar*.

Jacques Lezra, *On the Nature of Marx's Things: Translation as Necrophilology*.

Jean-Luc Nancy, *Portrait*. Translated by Sarah Clift and Simon Sparks, Introduction by Jeffrey S. Librett